Living Language™

CONVERSATIONAL PORTUGUESE

THE LIVING LANGUAGE COURSES®

Living Spanish
Living French
Living German
Living Japanese
Living Russian
Living Portuguese (South American)
Living Portuguese (Continental)
Living Hebrew
Living Swahili
Children's Living French
Children's Living Spanish
Advanced Living French
Advanced Living Spanish
Living English for Native Spanish Speakers
Living English for Native French Speakers
Living English for Native Italian Speakers
Living English for Native German Speakers
Living English for Native Portuguese Speakers
Living English for Native Chinese Speakers
Living Language™ Spanish Video
Living Language™ French Video
Living Language™ German Video

Additional Living Language™ conversation manuals
and dictionaries may be purchased separately.

Living Language™
CONVERSATIONAL PORTUGUESE

A COMPLETE COURSE IN EVERYDAY PORTUGUESE

by Oscar Fernández
DIRECTOR PORTUGUESE PROGRAM,
NEW YORK UNIVERSITY

BASED ON THE METHOD DEVISED BY
RALPH WEIMAN, FORMERLY CHIEF OF
LANGUAGE SECTION, U.S. WAR DEPARTMENT

SPECIALLY PREPARED FOR USE WITH
THE CONTINENTAL OR SOUTH AMERICAN
EDITION OF LIVING PORTUGUESE:
THE COMPLETE LIVING LANGUAGE COURSE®

Crown Publishers, Inc., New York

Published by Living Language, a division of Crown Publishers, Inc., 225 Park Avenue South, New York, New York 10003.

LIVING LANGUAGE is a trademark and THE LIVING LANGUAGE COURSE is a Registered Trademark of Crown Publishers, Inc.

Manufactured in the United States of America

Library of Congress Catalog Card Number: 65-22296

ISBN 0-517-56163-8

1986 Updated Edition

10 9 8 7 6 5 4 3 2 1

CONTENTS

INTRODUCTION   xi
INSTRUCTIONS   xv

BASIC PORTUGUESE VOCABULARY AND GRAMMAR

LESSON 1   1
  1. THE LETTERS AND SOUNDS   1

LESSON 2   4
(The Letters and Sounds Cont.)
  2. THE PORTUGUESE ALPHABET   7
  3. REGIONAL DIFFERENCES IN PRONUNCIATION   7

LESSON 3   8
  4. PRONUNCIATION PRACTICE   8

LESSON 4   12
(Pronunciation Practice Cont.)
  5. BUILDING UP A VOCABULARY   14

LESSON 5   17
  6. USEFUL WORD GROUPS   17

LESSON 6   21
  7. GOOD MORNING!   21
  8. WHERE IS . . . ?   24

LESSON 7   25
(Where Is . . . ? Cont.)
  9. DO YOU HAVE . . . ?   26
  10. WHAT DO YOU HAVE TO EAT?   27

LESSON 8   30
  11. SOME COMMON VERB FORMS   30
  12. "THE" AND "A"   33
  13. CONTRACTIONS   34

14. PLURAL   35
15. ADJECTIVES   36
16. POSSESSION   36
17. ASKING A QUESTION   37
18. "NO" AND "NOT"   37
19. INTRODUCTIONS   39
20. A GOOD TIME   40

LESSON 9   41
21. WHAT'S NEW?   41
22. TO BE OR NOT TO BE   43
23. IT IS   46

LESSON 10   47
24. TO HAVE AND HAVE NOT   47
25. I KNOW ONLY A LITTLE PORTUGUESE   48

LESSON 11   50
26. DO YOU SPEAK PORTUGUESE?   50
27. EXCUSE ME   53

LESSON 12   54
28. THIS AND THAT   54
29. MORE OR LESS   55
30. "AND" AND "BUT"   58

LESSON 13   59
31. WHERE?   59

LESSON 14   61
(Where? Cont.)
32. I, YOU, HE   64

LESSON 15   66
(I, You, He, Cont.)

LESSON 16   79
33. A FEW SHORT PHRASES   79
34. MAY I ASK?   80

LESSON 17   81
35. NUMBERS   81

LESSON 18   84
(Numbers Cont.)
36. HOW MUCH?   86
37. IT COSTS . . .   86
38. MY ADDRESS IS . . .   87
39. MY TELEPHONE NUMBER IS . . .   87
40. THE NUMBER IS . . .   87

LESSON 19   88
41. WHAT'S TODAY?   88
42. SOME DATES   89
43. WHAT TIME IS IT?   90

LESSON 20   91
(What Time Is It? Cont.)
44. IT'S TIME   92
45. PAST, PRESENT AND FUTURE   93
46. MORNING, NOON AND NIGHT   94

LESSON 21   94
(Morning, Noon and Night Cont.)

LESSON 22   100
47. NO   100

LESSON 23   102
(No Cont.)
48. USEFUL WORD GROUPS II   103

LESSON 24   106
(Useful Word Groups Cont.)
49. HAVE YOU TWO MET?   108
50. SMALL TALK   109

LESSON 25   110
(Small Talk Cont.)
51. TAKING LEAVE   110

LESSON 26   113
52. CALLING ON SOMEONE   113
53. LETTERS AND TELEGRAMS   114

LESSON 27   116
54. GETTING AROUND   116
55. PLEASE   118
56. SOME USEFUL EXPRESSIONS   120

LESSON 28   124
(Some Useful Expressions Cont.)
57. WHO? WHAT? WHEN?   124

LESSON 29   126
(Who? What? When? Cont.)
58. LIKING AND DISLIKING   131

LESSON 30   133
(Liking and Disliking Cont.)
59. IN, TO, FROM   136

LESSON 31   137
(In, To, From Cont.)

LESSON 32   143
60. ASKING YOUR WAY   143

LESSON 33   146
(Asking Your Way Cont.)
61. WRITING, PHONING, TELEGRAPHING   147

LESSON 34   150
62. FAMILY AFFAIRS   150

LESSON 35   155
63. COMPRAS (SHOPPING)   155
64. O CAFÉ DA MANHÃ ⑧ (O PEQUENO ALMOÇO ⑫)
(BREAKFAST)   161
65. CARDÁPIO ⑧ (EMENTA ⑫) A SAMPLE MENU   166

LESSON 36   166
66. PROCURANDO APARTAMENTO
(APARTMENT HUNTING)   166
67. SOME COMMON VERBS   174

LESSON 37   181
68. NÃO SOU DAQUI (I'M A STRANGER HERE)   181

LESSON 38   188
69. CUMPRIMENTANDO UM VELHO AMIGO
(GREETING AN OLD FRIEND)   188
70. THE MOST COMMON VERBS AND THEIR FORMS   197

LESSON 39   208
71. WHAT'S IN A NAME?   208

LESSON 40   211
72. PORTUGUESE IN A LIGHTER VEIN   211
73. IMPORTANT SIGNS   216

SUMMARY OF PORTUGUESE GRAMMAR

1. THE ALPHABET   223
2. PRONUNCIATION   223
3. STRESS   228
4. PUNCTUATION   228
5. SOME ORTHOGRAPHIC SIGNS   229
6. SYLLABLE DIVISION   231
7. THE DEFINITE ARTICLE   232
8. THE INDEFINITE ARTICLE   234
9. CONTRACTIONS   235
10. DAYS OF THE WEEK   236
11. THE NAMES OF THE MONTHS   237
12. THE NAMES OF THE SEASONS   237·
13. MASCULINE AND FEMININE   238
14. THE PLURAL   240
15. THE POSSESSIVE   241
16. ADJECTIVES   242
17. POSITION OF ADJECTIVES   244

18. COMPARISON | 246
19. PRONOUNS | 248
20. POSITIONS OF PRONOUNS | 252
21. SOME CONJUNCTIONS | 256
22. QUESTION WORDS | 257
23. ADVERBS | 258
24. DIMINUTIVES AND AUGMENTATIVES | 261
25. DEMONSTRATIVES | 263
26. INDEFINITE ADJECTIVES AND PRONOUNS | 265
27. NEGATION | 266
28. WORD ORDER | 266
29. THE INFINITIVE | 267
30. THE TENSES OF THE VERB | 268
31. THE SUBJUNCTIVE | 273
32. SEQUENCE OF TENSES | 278
33. THE CONDITIONAL | 279
34. CONDITIONAL SENTENCES | 281
35. COMMANDS AND REQUESTS | 282
36. THE PARTICIPLE | 286
37. PROGRESSIVE TENSES | 288
38. THE PASSIVE VOICE | 288
39. TO BE | 289
40. THE FORMS OF THE REGULAR VERB | 293
41. RADICAL-CHANGING VERBS | 299
42. SPELLING CHANGES IN VERBS | 302
43. IRREGULAR VERBS | 307

LETTER WRITING

1. FORMAL INVITATIONS AND REPLIES | 319
2. THANK-YOU NOTE | 322
3. BUSINESS LETTERS | 323
4. INFORMAL LETTERS | 326
5. USEFUL PHRASES FOR CORRESPONDENCE | 328
6. FORM OF THE ENVELOPE | 332

INTRODUCTION TO THE COMPLETE LIVING LANGUAGE COURSE®

The Living Language Course® uses the natural method of language-learning. You learn Portuguese the way you learned English—by hearing the language and repeating what you heard. You didn't begin by studying grammar; you first learned how to say things, how words are arranged, and only when you knew the language pretty well did you begin to study grammar. This course teaches you Portuguese in the same way. Hear it, say it, absorb it through use and repetition. The only difference is that in this course the basic elements of the language have been carefully selected and condensed into 40 short lessons. When you have finished these lessons, you will have a good working knowledge of the language. If you apply yourself, you can master this course and learn to speak basic Portuguese in a few weeks.

While *Living Language™ Conversational Portuguese* is designed for use with the South American or Continental editions of Living Portuguese: The Complete Living Language Course®, this book may be used without the cassettes. The first 4 lessons cover Portuguese pronunciation, laying the foundation for learning the vocabulary, phrases, and grammar that are explained in the later chapters.

All the material is presented in order of importance. When you reach page 150, you will have already learned 300 of the most frequently used sentences and will be able to make yourself understood on many important topics. By the time you have finished this course, you will have a sufficient command of Portuguese to get along in all ordinary situations.

The brief but complete summary of Portuguese grammar is included in the back of this book to enable you to perfect your knowledge of the language. There are also many other helpful features, such as vocabulary-building exercises and verb conjugations. The special section on letter-writing will show you how to answer an invitation, make a business inquiry, and address an envelope properly. Just as important is the *Living Language*™ *Common Usage Dictionary*. This is included in the course primarily for use as a reference, but it doubles as a phrasebook. It contains the most common Portuguese words with their meanings illustrated by everyday sentences and idiomatic expressions. The basic words—those you should learn from the start—are capitalized to make them easy to find.

Keep practicing your Portuguese as much as possible. Once you are well along in the course, try reading Portuguese magazines, newspapers, and books. Use your Portuguese whenever you get a chance—with Portuguese-speaking friends, with other students.

This course tries to make learning Portuguese as easy and enjoyable as possible, but a certain amount of application is necessary. The cassettes and books that make up this course provide you with all the material you need; the instructions tell you what to do. The rest is up to you.

SOUTH AMERICAN (Brazilian) vs. CONTINENTAL PORTUGUESE

Although the language spoken in Portugal and Brazil is the same language, there are certain differences, just as there are differences between British and American English. The structure of the language is much the same, but there are significant variations in word order, in pronunciation, and in intonation (see sections 3 and 4 of Lessons 2 and 3), and this makes alternate sets of recordings necessary, one in Brazilian Portuguese and one in Continental Portuguese.

To make it possible for *Conversational Portuguese* and the *Common Usage Dictionary* to be used with either edition, an effort has been made to use vocabulary and phrases common to both patterns. Otherwise, the basic pattern followed is the Brazilian, with significant variations in Continental Portuguese being indicated.

SPELLING

1. Following Brazilian usage, the text will have many accent marks which are no longer used in Portugal. This is particularly true of accent marks which appear on syllables which do not need them according to the rules for stress (see Lesson 1), but which Brazilians keep to distinguish words spelled alike but with different meanings (*almôço* lunch, and *almoço* I eat lunch), or for other reasons.

BRAZIL	PORTUGAL	MEANING
almôço	*almoço*	lunch
êle	*ele*	he
aquêle	*aquele*	that one

The first time such a form appears in the text, the variation used in Portugal will be given in parentheses or in a footnote, and will be marked ℗.

2. Differences in pronunciation, which require different spellings, and variants of the same word, although pronounced the same way in both countries, will also be given:

BRAZIL	PORTUGAL	MEANING
ação	acção	action
Antônio	António	Anthony
diretor	director	director
otimista	optimista	optimist

These variants will also be given in parentheses, or in a footnote, and will be marked ℗.

3. Other differences, as in vocabulary and word order, will be indicated in the same manner: *abacaxi (ananás ℗)* pineapple; *Eu me diverti (Eu divertime ℗)* I had a good time. At times ⓑ will be used to indicate a particularly Brazilian form: *marrom* ⓑ brown; *suetér* ⓑ sweater.

4. In some cases the use of certain words or forms is optional, and they may or may not be used: subject pronouns, the definite article (especially with possessives, and used more in Portugal than in Brazil—see Lesson 15), etc. These optional forms will sometimes be given in parentheses, and *Conversational Portuguese* will indicate differences between the two sets of recordings: *(Ela) chama-se Maria. É (a) minha irmã.* Her name is Mary. She is my sister.

5. In the *Living Language™ Common Usage Dictionary*, the Continental Portuguese variation will be given in parentheses. The designators ℗ and ⓑ will be used only when they seem necessary for clarity.

Course Material

The material of the complete Living Language Course® consists of the following:

1. *2 hour-long cassettes* or *4 long-playing records.* The label on each face indicates clearly which lessons are contained on that side. Living Portuguese is available in both Continental and South American (Brazilian) editions.

2. *Conversational Portuguese manual.* This book is designed for use with the recorded lessons, or it may be used alone. It contains the following sections:

   Basic Portuguese Vocabulary and Grammar
   Summary of Portuguese Grammar
   Letter Writing

3. *Portuguese-English/English-Portuguese Common Usage Dictionary.* A special kind of dictionary that gives you the literal translations of more than 18,000 Portuguese words, plus idiomatic phrases and sentences illustrating the everyday use of the more important vocabulary and 1,000 essential words capitalized for quick reference.

How to Use Conversational Portuguese with the Living Language™ Cassettes

TO BEGIN
There are 2 cassettes with 10 lessons per side. The beginning of each lesson is announced on the tape and each lesson takes approximately 3 minutes. If your cassette player has a digit indicator, you can locate any desired point precisely.

LEARNING THE LESSONS

1. Look at page 1. Note the words in **boldface** type. These are the words you will hear on the cassette. There are pauses to enable you to repeat each word and phrase right after you hear it.

2. Now read Lesson 1. (The ▭ ▭ symbols indicate the beginning of the recorded material. In some advanced lessons, information and instructions precede the recording.) Note the points to listen for when you play the cassette. Look at the first word: **Alberto,** and be prepared to follow the voice you will hear.

3. Play the cassette, listen carefully, and watch for the points mentioned. Then rewind, play the lesson again, and this time say the words aloud. Keep repeating until you are sure you know the lesson. The more times you listen and repeat, the longer you will remember the material.

4. Now go on to the next lesson. It's always good to quickly review the previous lesson before starting a new one.

5. There are 2 kinds of quizzes at the end of each section. One is the matching type, in which you must select the English translation of the Portuguese sentence. In the other, you fill in the blanks with the correct Portuguese word chosen from the 3 given directly below the sentence. Do these quizzes faithfully and, if you make any mistakes, reread the section.

6. When you get 100 percent on the Final Quiz, you may consider that you have mastered the course.

LESSON 1

1. THE LETTERS AND SOUNDS

(Letters and Sounds I)

A. Some Portuguese sounds are fairly similar to English sounds. Listen to and repeat the following Portuguese names and notice which sounds are fairly similar and which are different:

Alberto	Albert	**Júlio**	Julius
Alfredo	Alfred	**Lúcia**	Lucy
Ana	Anna, Anne	**Luís**	Louis
Antônio[1]	Anthony	**Manuel**	Manuel
Carlos	Charles	**Maria**	Mary
Cecília	Cecilia	**Mário**	Mario
Eduardo	Edward	**Maurício**	Maurice
Fernando	Ferdinand	**Miguel**	Michael
Francisco	Francis	**Paulo**	Paul
Glória	Gloria	**Pedro**	Peter
Guilherme	William	**Raimundo**	Raymond
Henrique	Henry	**Ricardo**	Richard
Isabel	Elizabeth	**Roberto**	Robert
João	John	**Rosa**	Rose
Jorge	George	**Tomás**	Thomas

NOTICE:

1. Each vowel is pronounced clearly and crisply.

2. A single consonant is pronounced with the following vowel.

---

[1] **António** Ⓟ.

3. The accent mark (´ or ˆ) indicates the syllable that is stressed: *Tomás*.

    (a) The acute accent mark (´) over *a, e, o* indicates an open pronunciation (in forming the sound there is a large opening between the roof of the mouth and the tongue): *Glória*.

    (b) The circumflex accent mark (ˆ) over *a, e, o* indicates a closed pronunciation (a smaller opening between the roof of the mouth and the tongue): *Pôrto (Porto* Ⓟ*)*.

4. The tilde (*til*) (˜) over a vowel indicates a nasal sound: *João*.

B. Now listen to the names of some cities:

Barcelona	Nova Iorque
Belém	Paris
Belo Horizonte	Pôrto[1]
Brasília	Pôrto Alegre[1]
Coimbra	Rio de Janeiro
Lisboa	Roma
Londres	Santos
Madrid	São Paulo

C. Now the names of some countries:

Alemanha (Germany)	Colômbia
Angola	Cuba
Argentina	Espanha (Spain)
Brasil	Estados Unidos (U.S.)
China	França

---

[1] Porto Ⓟ.
   Porto Alegre Ⓟ.

Inglaterra (England)   **Moçambique**
Itália   **Portugal**
México   **Uruguai**

Notice the following points (more detailed distinctions will be made later in the course):

VOWELS

a approximates *a* in *ah, father.*
e open, as explained above: *eh, best;* closed, approximates modified *a* as in *case;* compare *fez.*
i as in *machine.*
o open, as in *off;* closed, as in *rose.*
u approximates *u* in *rule.*

CONSONANTS AND CONSONANT GROUPS

ch as *ch* in *machine.*
h is never pronounced.
lh as *lli* in *million.*
m and **n** tend to nasalize the vowel before them; do not close your lips in pronouncing a final **m.**
nh as *ni* in *onion.*
s between vowels as *z,* or as *s* in *rose;* initial **s,** or **ss,** as *ss* in *lesson.*

STRESS

NOTICE:

1. Words ending in *a, e,* or *o* (or in one of these vowels and *s, m,* or *ns*) are stressed on the syllable before last:

casa   house
pobre   poor
americano   American
mesas   tables

homem	man
homens	men

2. Words ending in any other letter, including nasal vowels and diphthongs (two vowels pronounced in union) are stressed on the last syllable:

aqui	here
peru	turkey
manhã	morning
papel	paper
falar	to speak
descansei	I rested

3. Words not following the above rules have a written accent mark which indicates the stressed syllable:

café	coffee
difícil	difficult
português	Portuguese
pássaro	bird
júri	jury

LESSON 2

D. Now listen to and repeat the following words which are similar in English and Portuguese. Notice how Portuguese spelling and pronunciation differ from English:

(Letters and Sounds II)

acompanhar	to accompany	atenção	attention
agente	agent	caso	case

centro	center	raça	race
cheque	check	restaurante	restaurant
certo	certain	silêncio	silence
celebrar	to celebrate	surprêsa[1]	surprise
diferente	different	teatro	theatre
difícil	difficult	exemplo	example
importante	important	garantir	to guarantee
interessante	interesting	geral	general
necessário	necessary	telefone	telephone
possível	possible	tipo	type
qualidade	quality	visita	visit

CONSONANTS

Notice the following points:

1. *c* before *a*, *o*, and *u*, and before any other consonant is like *c* in *cat:*

carta	letter
secreto	secret *(adj.)*

2. *c* before *e* and *i* is like the *c* in *center:*

cena	scene
sincero	sincere

3. *ç* (used only before *a*, *o*, or *u*) is like the *c* in *face:*

moço	young man
nação	nation

4. *g* before *e* and *i* is like the *s* in *measure:*

gente	people
gíria	slang

---

[1] surpresa Ⓟ.

5. otherwise *g* is like *g* in *go:*

gato   cat

6. *j* is similar to *g* before *e* and *i:*

jantar   to dine

7. *l* in Portuguese is formed with the tongue forward, the tip near the upper teeth:

livro   book
paletó   jacket (man's)

8. final *l* is quite soft:

Brasil   Brazil
mal   evil

9. *qu* before *a* or *o* is like *qu* in *quota:*

quadro   picture

10. *qu* before *e* or *i* is usually like *k:*

Quê?   What?
barquinha   small boat

11. *x* has the following sounds:

like *z:*
exame   examination
êxito   success

like *sh:*
caixa   box
mexer   to mix
xícara   cup

like *s* in *see:*
máximo   maximum

próximo next

like *x* in *wax:*

táxi taxi

sexo sex

2. THE PORTUGUESE ALPHABET

Letter	Name	Letter	Name	Letter	Name
a	**a**	i	**i**	r	**erre**
b	**bê**	j	**jota**	s	**esse**
c	**cê**	l	**ele**	t	**tê**
d	**dê**	m	**eme**	u	**u**
e	**é**	n	**ene**	v	**vê**
f	**efe**	o	**ó**	x	**xis**
g	**gê**	p	**pê**	z	**zê**
h	**agá**	q	**quê**		

3. REGIONAL DIFFERENCES IN PRONUNCIATION

A language will vary somewhat in different countries where it is spoken, indeed, even in different parts of the same country. This is true of Portuguese.

Brazil, fifth largest country in size in the world, has been attaining increased importance. It comprises about one-half of the continent of South America and accounts for about one-half of its total population. Its language is Portuguese, but with certain features which distinguish it from the language as spoken in Portugal. There are also some minor regional differences in Brazil itself. The *carioca* pattern of Rio de Janeiro (whose inhabitants are called *cariocas*) is quite distinctive. Farther south, as in São Paulo, and in the northern part of the country one notices further minor differences, but basically the language is the same in all these cases.

The Portuguese language as spoken in Portugal is fundamentally the same language as is spoken in Brazil, but there are minor differences in syntax and significantly marked variations in pronunciation, intonation and rhythm. Syllables are cut shorter and at times slurred over, with final vowels clipped sharply or practically dropped.

LESSON 3

4. PRONUNCIATION PRACTICE

(Pronunciation Practice I)

The following groups of words will give you an idea of some of the regional differences in pronunciation and will also provide additional practice in Portuguese pronunciation and spelling. The first pronunciation is as in São Paulo, the second as in Rio de Janeiro, and the third as in Portugal.

CONSONANTS

1. *d* is pronounced more forcefully in Rio de Janeiro and with some speakers approximates the *j* in *just;* this is especially true with *d* before *e* or *i*:

São Paulo	Rio	Portugal	
cidade	**cidade**	**cidade**	city
Bom dia.	**Bom dia.**	**Bom dia.**	Good morning.

2. *r* is pronounced with the tongue forward, along the top of the mouth with the tip near the base of the upper teeth (as in Spanish), with initial *r* and *rr* being more forceful, with the tongue vibrating in this position. This pronunciation can be heard in São Paulo and in Portugal.

The *carioca r* is pronounced back in the mouth, the upper back part of the tongue against the roof of the mouth (similar to a French back *r* and somewhat like *ch* in German).

São Paulo	*Rio*	*Portugal*	
caro	**caro**	**caro**	expensive
carro	**carro**	**carro**	car, cart
Rio	**Rio**	**Rio**	Rio

3. *s* between vowels is as *z* in *zeal,* or as *s* in *rose:*

fase	**fase**	**fase**	phase

s before a voiced consonant (produced with a vibration of the vocal cords, as *b, d, ge, gi, j, l, m, n, r, v, z*) tends to be as *z* in *azure,* as Portuguese *j:*

mesmo	**mesmo**	**mesmo**	same
Lisboa	**Lisboa**	**Lisboa**	Lisbon

Final *s* and *s* (and *x*) before a voiceless consonant (produced without a vibration of the vocal cords, as hard *c* and hard *g, f, p, qu, t*) are pronounced as *s* in *see* in São Paulo and by some *cariocas,* and as *sh* in *shine* in Portugal and by some *cariocas:*

costas	**costas**	**costas**	coasts
prosperidade	**prosperidade**	**prosperidade**	prosperity
môscas	**môscas**	**moscas** Ⓟ	flies

4. Initial *s*, *s* after a consonant, and *ss*, as *s* in *see*, as *ss* in *passage:*

sempre	**sempre**	**sempre**	always
falso	**falso**	**falso**	false
passar	**passar**	**passar**	to pass

5. *t* before *e* or *i* is pronounced very forcefully by some *cariocas*, approximating the *ch* in *church:*

tinteiro	**tinteiro**	**tinteiro**	inkwell

VOWELS

1. *a* in a stressed position is "open" like the *a* in *father;* in unstressed positions and with the article *a* ("the") it tends to be more "closed" like the final *a* in *America;* this is particularly true in Portugal and in general with unstressed final *a:*

matar	**matar**	**matar**	to kill
a data	**a data**	**a data**	the date

2. *e*, in addition to the pronunciation indicated in Lesson 1, in a final unstressed position varies between the *i* in *did* and the *i* in *machine* in Brazil; it is clipped sharply in Portugal, being like a mute *e*, or is dropped:

breve	**breve**	**breve**	brief
verdade	**verdade**	**verdade**	truth

Stressed *e* before *j*, *ch*, *lh*, *nh* in Portugal can have the sound of final *a* in *America*, or of closed *e:*

cereja	**cereja**	**cereja**	cherry
igreja	**igreja**	**igreja**	church
fecha	**fecha**	**fecha**	he closes
venho	**venho**	**venho**	I come

e in an unstressed position is sometimes pronounced as *e* in *be,* in parts of Brazil, as mute *e* in Portugal, or as *i* in *did* in both:

exercício	exercício	exercício	exercise
devagar	devagar	devagar	slowly
pedir	pedir	pedir	to ask
respeito	respeito	respeito	respect

3. *o,* in addition to the pronunciation already indicated in Lesson 1 ("open" as *o* in *off,* and "closed" as *o* in *oh*), is also pronounced like *oo* in *boot* in an unstressed position, quite regularly in Portugal, and less consistently in Brazil (for example, less so in São Paulo than in Rio de Janeiro); this applies also to the pronunciation of the definite article *o* ("the"), and to *o* in a final unstressed position:

todos	todos	todos	all
o movimento	o movimento	o movimento	
the movement			
os portuguêses	os portuguêses	os portugueses Ⓟ	
the Portuguese			

LESSON 4

(Pronunciation Practice II)

NASAL SOUNDS

1. *m, n,* and *nh,* nasal sounds, tend to nasalize the vowel preceding them; this nasal quality is especially strong in Brazil; in Continental Portuguese it may be slight or even absent:

campo	field	**nome**	name
tentar	to try	**menos**	less
cama	bed	**pomada**	pomade
linha	line	**senhorita**	miss, young lady

m, n followed by a consonant are not pronounced, nor in final position (do not close your lips in pronouncing final *m;* merely nasalize the preceding vowel):

cantar	to sing	**falam**	they speak
também	also	**tem**	he has
sempre	always	**bom**	good
bomba	bomb	**um**	a, one

2. *ã, õ* are nasalized:

lã	wool	**manhã**	morning

3. nasal vowel combinations:

mãe	mother	**lições**	lessons
mão	hand	**põe**	he puts

4. a special case: **muito**   much

SOME OTHER VOWEL COMBINATIONS

1. *ai:* **pai**   father

2. *au:* **aula** class **causa** cause
3. *ei:* **falei** I spoke **sei** I know
   éi: **hotéis** hotels **papéis** papers
4. *eu:* **meu** my, mine
   escreveu he wrote
   éu: **céu** sky **chapéu** hat
5. *ia:* **diálogo** dialogue
6. *ie:* **série** series
   ié: **dieta** diet
7. *io:* **próprio** proper, (one's) own
8. *iu:* **partiu** he left
9. *oi:* **noite** night **coisa** thing
   ói: **herói** hero
   lençóis sheets (of bed)
10. *ou:* **outro** another, other
    comprou he bought
11. *ua:* **água** water **quando** when
12. *ué:* **suéter** Ⓑ sweater
13. *ui:* **cuidar** to take care (of)
14. *uo:* **quota** quota

WORD GROUPS

Keep in mind that the information given about pronunciation applies to word groups as well as to individual words:

1. *s* between vowels is like *z* in *zeal:*

todososamigos all the friends
(todos os amigos)

2. voiced *s* before a voiced consonant is like *z* in *azure:*

osdemais the rest
(os demais)

3. and so in other cases.

RHYTHM AND INTONATION

To speak Portuguese well you should not only pronounce individual words and word groups correctly, but you should try to use the proper rhythm and intonation. Pay attention to these and try to imitate them in the following examples.

1. In a declarative statement the tone level is normal, with a slight drop at the end:

A escola está aberta.   The school is open.
A escola está aberta.

2. In a question there is a slight rise at the end:

A escola está aberta?   Is the school open?
A escola está aberta?

3. Compare: **Êle[1] está aqui?**   **Êle está aqui.**
                   Is he here?   He is here.

          Êle está aqui?   **Êle está aqui.**

4. Exclamations and phrases said with emotion will affect inflection and may show a rise at the end:

Êle está ferido!   He is wounded (hurt)!
Êle está ferido!
Não me diga!   You don't say!
Não me diga!

5. BUILDING UP A VOCABULARY

Building up a Portuguese vocabulary is facilitated by the great number of words that are similar in English and Portuguese. Some words are spelled exactly the same (although they may differ considerably in pronunciation):

---

[1] **Ele** Ⓟ.

PORTUGUESE	ENGLISH	PORTUGUESE	ENGLISH
animal	animal	*hospital*	hospital
capital	capital	*hotel*	hotel
central	central	*motor*	motor
chocolate	chocolate	*original*	original
envelope	˙envelope	*regular*	regular
favor	favor	*total*	total

There are many Portuguese words which you will have no difficulty in recognizing despite minor differences. Some of these differences are:

a. The Portuguese word has an accent mark:

área	area	*júnior*	junior
cônsul	consul	*rádio*	radio

b. The Portuguese word has a single consonant:

antena	antenna	*comercial*	commercial
anual	annual	*oficial*	official

c. The Portuguese word adds -*a*, -*e*, or -*o*:

lista	list	*problema*	problem
mapa	map	*restaurante*	restaurant
parte	part	*revolta*	revolt

d. The Portuguese word ends in *a* or *o*, the English word in *e*:

causa	cause	*nota*	note
figura	figure	*rosa*	rose
medicina	medicine	*tubo*	tube
minuto	minute	*uso*	use

e. The Portuguese word is slightly different in other respects:

automóvel	automobile	*origem*	origin
especial	special	*questão*	question

GENERAL EQUIVALENTS

1. Portuguese *c* (*qu*) = English *k* (*ck*):

| *franco* | frank | *ataque* | attack |
| *parque* | park | *saco* | sack |

2. Portuguese *f* = English *ph:*

| *filosofia* | philosophy | *frase* | phrase, sentence |
| *físico* | physical | *telefone* | telephone |

3. Portuguese *t* = English *th:*

| *autor* | author | *simpatia* | sympathy |
| *autoridade* | authority | *teatro* | theatre |

4. Portuguese *ç* = English *ce:*

| *fôrça*[1] | force | *raça* | race |

5. Portuguese *i* = English *y:*

| *estilo* | style | *ritmo* | rhythm |
| *mistério* | mystery | *sistema* | system |

6. Portuguese *o* and *u* = English *ou:*

côrte[2]	court	*sopa*	soup
hora	hour	*anunciar*	to announce
montanha	mountain	*curso*	course
som	sound	*fundar*	to found

7. Portuguese *-ia* and *-io* = English *y:*

companhia	company	*secretária*	secretary
família	family	*remédio*	remedy
história	history, story	*território*	territory

---

[1] *força* Ⓟ.
[2] *corte* Ⓟ.

8. Portuguese *-ia, -a,* and *-o* = English *e:*

ausência	absence	*diferença*	difference
distância	distance	*justiça*	justice
experiência	experience	*comércio*	commerce
notícia	notice, news	*silêncio*	silence
polícia	police	*serviço*	service

9. Portuguese *-ção* = English *-tion:*

atenção	attention	*imitação*	imitation
cooperação	cooperation	*informação*	information
descrição	description	*satisfação*	satisfaction
estação	station	*tradução*	translation

10. Portuguese *-o* = English *-al:*

eterno	eternal	*político*	political

11. Portuguese *-oso* = English *-ous:*

delicioso	delicious	*famoso*	famous
numeroso	numerous	*religioso*	religious

12. Portuguese *-dade* = English *-ty:*

cidade	city	*possibilidade*	possibility
oportunidade	opportunity	*qualidade*	quality

LESSON 5

6. USEFUL WORD GROUPS

(Useful Word Groups I)

NUMBERS

um *(masc.)*, **uma** *(fem.)* one
dois *(masc.)*, **duas** *(fem.)* two

três	three
quatro	four
cinco	five
seis	six
sete	seven
oito	eight
nove	nine
dez	ten

THE DAYS OF THE WEEK

segunda-feira or **segunda**	Monday
têrça-feira or **têrça**[1]	Tuesday
quarta-feira or **quarta**	Wednesday
quinta-feira or **quinta**	Thursday
sexta-feira or **sexta**	Friday
sábado	Saturday
domingo	Sunday

THE MONTHS

janeiro[2]	January
fevereiro	February
março	March
abril	April
maio	May
junho	June
julho	July
agôsto (Agosto)	August
setembro	September
outubro	October
novembro	November
dezembro	December

---

[1] **têrça-feira** or **têrça** Ⓟ.
[2] With initial capital letters in Portugal: **Janeiro,** etc.

SOME COLORS

vermelho	red
azul	blue
verde	green
prêto,[1] negro	black
branco	white
amarelo	yellow
castanho, marrom Ⓑ	brown
cinzento, gris Ⓑ	gray

THE SEASONS

a primavera[2]	spring
o verão	summer
o outono	autumn
o inverno	winter

NORTH, SOUTH, EAST, WEST

norte	north
sul	south
leste	east
oeste	west

MORNING, NOON AND NIGHT

manhã	morning
meio-dia	noon
tarde	afternoon
noite	evening, night

---

[1]preto Ⓟ.
[2]With initial capital letters in Portugal: **Primavera,** etc.

TODAY, YESTERDAY, TOMORROW

hoje	today
ontem	yesterday
amanhã	tomorrow

Hoje é sexta-feira.	Today is Friday.
Ontem foi quinta-feira.	Yesterday was Thursday.
Amanhã é sábado.	Tomorrow is Saturday.
Um mais um: dois.[1]	One and one are two.
Um mais dois: três.	One and two are three.
Dois mais dois: quatro.	Two and two are four.
Dois mais três: cinco.	Two and three are five.
Três mais três: seis.	Three and three are six.
Três mais quatro: sete.	Three and four are seven.
Quatro mais quatro: oito.	Four and four are eight.
Quatro mais cinco: nove.	Four and five are nine.
Cinco mais cinco: dez.	Five and five are ten.

QUIZ 1

Try matching these two columns:

1. sexta-feira	1. January
2. outono	2. summer
3. quinta-feira	3. June
4. primavera	4. winter
5. oito	5. October
6. janeiro	6. white

---

[1]This form is good for oral use. Another form: *Um mais um igual a dois,* etc.

7. *inverno*	7. autumn
8. *verde*	8. Sunday
9. *junho*	9. eight
10. *verão*	10. spring
11. *segunda-feira*	11. west
12. *quatro*	12. Thursday
13. *outubro*	13. four
14. *domingo*	14. ten
15. *oeste*	15. red
16. *vermelho*	16. black
17. *prêto*	17. green
18. *dez*	18. Friday
19. *branco*	19. gray
20. *cinzento*	20. Monday

ANSWERS

1—18; 2—7; 3—12; 4—10; 5—9; 6—1; 7—4; 8—17;
9—3; 10—2; 11—20; 12—13; 13—5; 14—8; 15—11;
16—15; 17—16; 18—14; 19—6; 20—19.

LESSON 6

7. GOOD MORNING!

(Good morning!)

De manhã	In the morning
bom	good
dia	day
Bom dia.	Good morning.
senhor	Mr.
Campos	Campos

Bom dia, senhor (Sr.) Campos.	Good morning, Mr. Campos.
como	how
vai (está)	are (you) getting along
o senhor [1]	you
Como vai (está) o senhor?	How are you?
muito	very
bem	well
Muito bem.	Very well.
obrigado	thank you
Muito bem, obrigado.	Very well, thank you.
e	and
o senhor	you
E o senhor?	And you?
bem	well
Bem, obrigado.	Fine, thank you.
De tarde	In the afternoon
boa	good
tarde	afternoon
Boa tarde.	Good afternoon.
Boa tarde, Dona Maria.	Good afternoon, Dona Maria.
Como vai (está) a senhora?	How are you?
Muito bem, obrigada. [2]	Very well, thank you.

[1] "You" is translated by *o senhor (masc.)* and *a senhora (fem.)* and by their plural forms *os senhores* and *as senhoras*.

[2] A man answers *obrigado*, a lady *obrigada*, for "thank you." Mr. and Mrs. Campos, *o senhor Campos e a senhora Campos;* however, it is more common to address a married woman by *Dona* and her first name: *Dona Maria*, etc.

E o senhor?	And you?
Muito bem, obrigado.	Very well, thank you.

De noite	In the evening
boa	good
noite	evening, night
Boa noite, Cecília.	Good evening, Cecilia.
Boa noite, Pedro.	Good evening, Peter.
Boa noite, Dona Maria.	Good evening, Dona Maria.
Boa noite, Pedro.	Good evening, Peter.

QUIZ 2

1. manhã	1. Good afternoon.
2. senhora	2. in the morning
3. Como vai (está) o senhor?	3. and
4. Muito bem.	4. morning
5. Bom dia.	5. Thank you.
6. Boa noite.	6. Mrs.
7. de manhã	7. Peter
8. tarde	8. Sir or Mr.
9. Obrigado.	9. How?
10. Pedro	10. Good morning.
11. e	11. in the evening
12. Boa tarde.	12. How are you?
13. Como?	13. Very well. (Fine.)
14. senhor	14. afternoon
15. de noite	15. Good evening. Good night.

ANSWERS

1—4; 2—6; 3—12; 4—13; 5—10; 6—15; 7—2; 8—14;
9—5; 10—7; 11—3; 12—1; 13—9; 14—8; 15—11.

8. WHERE IS . . . ?

onde	where
há	is there (there is)
Onde há . . . ?	Where is there . . . ?
um	a
hotel	hotel
Onde há um hotel?	Where is there a hotel?
bom	good
restaurante	restaurant
Onde há um bom restaurante?	Where is there a good restaurant?
onde	where
é	is
Onde é?	Where is it?
Onde é a Prefeitura (a Câmara Municipal Ⓟ)?	Where is the City Hall?
Onde é o restaurante?	Where is the restaurant?
Onde é a estação?	Where is the station?
Onde é o correio?	Where is the post office?

Note: There is a tendency to use *ser* with fixed location.

LESSON 7

▭▭

(What Do You Have To Eat?)

o senhor pode	can you
dizer-me	tell me
O senhor pode dizer-me...?	Can you tell me...?
O senhor pode dizer-me onde há um hotel?	Can you tell me where there is a hotel?
O senhor pode dizer-me onde há um bom restaurante?	Can you tell me where there is a good restaurant?
O senhor pode dizer-me onde é a Prefeitura (a Câmara Municipal)?	Can you tell me where the City Hall is?
O senhor pode dizer-me onde é a estação?	Can you tell me where the station is?
O senhor pode dizer-me onde é o correio?	Can you tell me where the post office is?

QUIZ 3

1. *Onde há um hotel?*
2. *Onde é a Prefeitura (a Câmara Municipal)?*
3. *O senhor pode dizer-me...?*

1. Where is the City Hall?
2. Can you tell me where the station is?
3. Can you tell me...?

4. *O Senhor pode dizer-*
me onde é a estação?

4. the post office

5. *o correio*

5. Where is there a
hotel?

ANSWERS

1—5; 2—1; 3—3; 4—2; 5—4.

9. DO YOU HAVE . . . ?

O senhor tem . . . ?	Do you have . . . ?
dinheiro	(any) money
cigarros	(any) cigarettes
fósforos	(any) matches
fogo (lume Ⓟ)	a light
Preciso de . . .	I need . . .
papel	(some paper)
lápis	(a) pencil
tinta	ink
um sêlo[1]	a (postage) stamp
sabonete	soap
pasta de dente (dentes)	toothpaste
uma toalha	a towel

_____

Onde posso comprar . . . ?	Where can I buy . . . ?
um dicionário português	a Portuguese dictionary

_____

[1] **selo** Ⓟ.

um dicionário inglês-português	an English-Portuguese dictionary
alguns livros em inglês	some English books ("some books in English")
algumas roupas	(some) clothes

10. WHAT DO YOU HAVE TO EAT?

o café da manhã (o pequeno or primeiro almoço	breakfast
o almôço	lunch
o jantar	dinner

O que é que o senhor deseja?	What will you have? ("What do you wish?")
faça o favor de	please ("do the favor of ")
dar-me	give me ("to give me")
o menu (a ementa Ⓟ)	the menu
Faça o favor de dar-me o menu (a ementa Ⓟ).	May I have a menu, please?

Temos ...	We have ...
pão	bread
pão e manteiga	bread and butter
sopa	soup
carne	meat
carne de vaca	beef

bife	steak (beefsteak)
carne de porco	pork
presunto	ham
peixe	fish
bacalhau	cod
camarão, camarões	shrimp *(sing. and plural)*
lagosta	lobster
sardinhas	sardines
frango	chicken
arroz	rice
ovos	eggs
ovos estrelados	fried eggs
ovos mexidos	scrambled eggs
verduras (legumes)	vegetables
milho	corn
batatas	potatoes
feijão	beans
salada	salad
salada de alface	lettuce salad
tomates	tomatoes
água	water
vinho	wine
cerveja	beer
leite	milk
café com leite	coffee with milk
açúcar	sugar
sal	salt
pimenta	pepper
frutas	fruit
abacaxi (ananás Ⓟ)	pineapple
bananas	banana
laranjas	oranges
maçãs	apples
sobremesa	dessert

Traga-me . . .	Bring me . . .
uma xícara de café (uma chávena de café)	a cup of coffee
uma xícara (chávena) de chá	a cup of tea
um guardanapo	a napkin
uma colher	a spoon
uma colher de chá	a teaspoon
uma faca	a knife
um prato	a plate
um copo	a glass
Gostaria de ter . . .	I would like to have . . .
uma garrafa de vinho	a bottle of wine
uma garrafa de cerveja	a bottle of beer
um chope (uma caneca Ⓟ*)*	draught beer
um cafèzinho Ⓑ	a small cup of coffee (demitasse)
mais uma garrafa	another bottle
um pouco mais disso	a little more of that
mais pão	more bread
A conta, faz favor.	The check, please.

QUIZ 4

1. *carne*	1. fish
2. *batatas*	2. water
3. *água*	3. vegetables
4. *O que é que o senhor deseja?*	4. I need soap.
5. *ovos*	5. The check, please.
6. *frango*	6. breakfast
7. *peixe*	7. a spoon
8. *uma garrafa de vinho*	8. coffee with milk

9. *Preciso de sabonete.*	9. What will you have?
10. *Traga-me pão.*	10. dessert
11. *café com leite*	11. meat
12. *açúcar*	12. a knife
13. *verduras (legumes)*	13. eggs
14. *uma xícara de chá*	14. Bring me some bread.
15. *um pouco mais de pão*	15. chicken
16. *uma faca*	16. a cup of tea
17. *sobremesa*	17. some more bread
18. *o café da manhã (o pequeno almoço)*	18. sugar
19. *uma colher*	19. a bottle of wine
20. *A conta, faz favor.*	20. potatoes

ANSWERS

1—11; 2—20; 3—2; 4—9; 5—13; 6—15; 7—1; 8—19; 9—4; 10—14; 11—8; 12—18; 13—3; 14—16; 15—17; 16—12; 17—10; 18—6; 19—7; 20—5.

LESSON 8

11. SOME COMMON VERB FORMS

(Introductions)

This lesson and several that follow are longer than the others. They contain information about grammar you need to know from the start. Try to understand each point, and as the course continues observe examples of the points mentioned. Refer back to the sections on grammar as often as necessary. Try to develop an understanding and feeling for the basic features of Portuguese grammar rather than a mere memorization of "rules."

SINGULAR

eu falo	I speak
(tu falas)	you speak *(familiar)*
êle[1] fala	he speaks
ela fala	she speaks
o senhor fala	you speak *(masc.)*
a senhora fala	you speak *(fem.)*
você fala	you speak

PLURAL

nós falamos	we speak
(vós falais)	(you speak)
êles[1] falam	they speak *(masc.)*
elas falam	they speak *(fem.)*
os senhores falam	you speak *(masc.)*
as senhoras falam	you speak *(fem.)*
vocês falam	you speak

The forms in parentheses are generally to be avoided.

NOTES

1. These forms, which make up the present tense, translate English "I speak," "I am speaking," "I do speak."

2. *Tu* "you" is used in very familiar speech, as between members of a family, and between very close friends. It is used much less in Brazil than in Portugal, Brazilians tending to use *você* in cases not calling for *o senhor* or *a senhora*. The plural *vós* is rarely used in Brazil today, being considered fairly archaic, *vocês* generally taking

---

[1] ele, eles Ⓟ.

its place in Portugal and in Brazil. *O senhor, a senhora,* and their plural forms are the "polite" or less "familiar" forms.

3. Notice that there are six endings:

Singular

—o	indicates the speaker (I).
(—as)	indicates the person spoken to (you). It is the familiar form.
—a	indicates someone or something spoken about (he, she, it), or spoken to (you).

Plural

—amos	indicates several people including the speaker (we).
(—ais)	indicates the persons spoken to (you). *This form is rarely used.*
—am	indicates those spoken about (they), or spoken to (you, *plural*).

4. Notice that the verb form used with *êle, ela, o senhor, a senhora,* and *você* is the same: *fala.* The plurals of these have the same form: *falam.*

5. Notice that several forms of the subject pronouns differ depending on whether men or women are speaking or are being spoken about:[1]

êle fala	he speaks
ela fala	she speaks
êles falam	they speak *(men)*
elas falam	they speak *(women)*

---

[1] This is also true when the pronouns refer to masculine or feminine nouns (see section 13 of Portuguese Grammar Summary).

12. "THE" AND "A"

1. The

o menino	the boy	*os meninos*	the boys
a menina	the girl	*as meninas*	the girls

Notice that the word for "the" is in some cases *o* (plural: *os*), in other cases *a* (plural: *as*). Nouns that take *o* are called "masculine," nouns that take *a* are called "feminine." Nouns referring to males are masculine, nouns referring to females are feminine. In the case of other nouns you should learn the gender of the noun, that is, whether it is masculine or feminine.

2. A (an)

um menino	a boy
uma menina	a girl
uns meninos	some (a few) boys
umas meninas	some (a few) girls

QUIZ 5

1. eu	1. they speak *(masc.)*
2. nós	2. she speaks
3. o senhor fala	3. she
4. êle	4. you speak (to friends, *plural*)
5. êles falam	5. I
6. vocês falam	6. you speak *(masc. sing. "polite")*
7. as senhoras falam	7. he

8. *ela*   8. we speak
9. *nós falamos*   9. you speak (*fem. pl.*
                              "polite")
10. *ela fala*   10. we

ANSWERS

1—5; 2—10; 3—6; 4—7; 5—1; 6—4; 7—9; 8—3;
9—8; 10—2.

13. CONTRACTIONS

de+o=do	*de+os=dos*	of the, from the
de+a=da	*de+as=das*	
a+o=ao	*a+os=aos*	to the
a+a=à	*a+as=às*	
em+o=no	*em+os=nos*	in the, on the
em+a=na	*em+as=nas*	

---

do menino	of the boy
da menina	of the girl
dos meninos	of the boys
das meninas	of the girls
ao menino	to the boy
à menina	to the girl
aos meninos	to the boys
às meninas	to the girls
no bôlso (bolso ℗).	in the pocket
nos bolsos	in the pockets
na praia	on the beach
nas praias	on the beaches

Contractions of *de* and *em* with the indefinite article (*um* and its other forms) are optional, both contracted forms and noncontracted forms being used:

de um menino or *dum menino*	of a boy
de uma escola or *duma escola*	of a school
em umas cidades or *numas cidades*	in some cities

14. PLURAL

1. Words ending in a vowel, including nasal vowels, or in a diphthong, usually add *s* to form the plural:

o galo	the rooster	*os galos*	the roosters
a maçã	the apple	*as maçãs*	the apples
a lei	the law	*as leis*	the laws

2. Feminine words ending in -*ão* usually end in -*ões* in the plural:

a civilização   civilization

as civilizações   civilizations

Masculine words in -*ão* usually end in -*ões* in the plural:

o coração   the heart   *os corações*   the hearts

However, some end in -*ãos* or in -*ães:*

cristão	Christian	*cristãos*	Christians
alemão	German	*alemães*	Germans

3. Words ending in -*r* or -*z* add *es:*

a flor	the flower	*as flôres*[1]	the flowers
a voz	the voice	*as vozes*	the voices

---

[1] *as flores* Ⓟ.

4. Words ending in *-al, -el, -ol,* or *-ul* drop the *l* and
add *is:*

o jornal	the newspaper	*os jornais*	the newspapers
amável	pleasant, nice	*amáveis (pl.)*	

15. ADJECTIVES

o aluno alto	the tall student *(masc.)*
a aluna alta	the tall student *(fem.)*
os alunos altos	the tall students *(masc.)*
as alunas altas	the tall students *(fem.)*

Notice that a descriptive adjective tends to follow
the noun it modifies and agrees with it in gender
and number, that is, it is masculine if the noun is
masculine, plural if the noun is plural, etc.

The adjective, used without the noun, indicates
through its form whether the noun referred to is
masculine or feminine, and whether it is singular or
plural:

(êle) É espanhol.	He's Spanish.
(ela) É espanhola.	She's Spanish.
(êles) São espanhóis.	They're Spanish. *(masc.)*
(elas) São espanholas.	They're Spanish. *(fem.)*

16. POSSESSION

English *-'s* or *-s'* is translated by *de* "of":

a caneta do João	John's pen ("the pen of John")
os cadernos dos professôres[1]	the professors' notebooks ("the notebooks of the professors")

---

[1]*professores* Ⓟ.

17. ASKING A QUESTION

1. To ask a question, use the same word order as for a statement, but change the intonation (this is the more common form, especially in Brazil):

O senhor chegou cedo.   You arrived early.
O senhor chegou cedo?   Did you arrive early?

2. The word order may be inverted, with the verb before the subject:

Chegou o senhor cedo?   Did you arrive early?

18. "NO" AND "NOT"

The word for "no" and for "not" is *não*. To make a statement negative put *não* before the verb:

Não vejo.   I don't see.

REVIEW QUIZ 1

1. *Boa* ____ (afternoon), *senhor Coelho.*
   a. *manhã*
   b. *tarde*
   c. *obrigada*

2. *Pode dizer-me* ____ (where) *é o correio?*
   a. *onde*
   b. *bom*
   c. *quando*

3. ____ (bring me) *pão.*
   a. *deseja*
   b. *chegou*
   c. *traga-me*

4. *Café com* ____ (milk).
   a. *açúcar*
   b. *vinho*
   c. *leite*

5. *Um pouco* ____ (more) *de carne.*
   a. *mais*
   b. *copo*
   c. *outro*

6. *No dia sete de* ____ (January).
   a. *março (Março Ⓟ)*
   b. *janeiro (Janeiro Ⓟ)*
   c. *outubro (Outubro Ⓟ)*

7. ____ (Wednesday), *cinco de setembro.*
   a. *sexta-feira*
   b. *sábado*
   c. *quarta-feira*

8. ____ (how) *vai (está) o senhor?*
   a. *amável*
   b. *como*
   c. *cedo*

9. *Boa* ____ (evening), *Dona Maria.*
   a. *com*
   b. *noite*
   c. *eu*

10. *Traga-me uma garrafa de* ____ (wine).
    a. *chá*
    b. *vinho*
    c. *água*

ANSWERS

1b; 2a; 3c; 4c; 5a; 6b; 7c; 8b; 9b; 10b.

19. INTRODUCTIONS

Bom dia.	Good morning.
Bom dia, senhor.	Good morning, sir.
Como vai?	How are you?
Muito bem, obrigado.	Very well, thank you.
E o senhor? O senhor é americano?	How are you? Are you (an) American?
Sim, senhor.	Yes (sir).
O senhor fala português?	Do you speak Portuguese?
Um pouco.	A little.

quero	I want
apresentar-lhe	to introduce to you
(a) minha amiga	my friend
Glória Santos	Gloria Santos
Quero apresentar-lhe (a) minha amiga, Glória Santos.	I want to introduce to you my friend, Gloria Santos.

muito prazer	much pleasure
Muito prazer.	I'm glad to know you.
o prazer	the pleasure
é todo meu	is all mine
O prazer é todo meu.	The pleasure is all mine.

permita-me	allow me
apresentar-me	to introduce myself
João Silva	John Silva
Permita-me apresentar-me. João Silva.	May I introduce myself? I'm John Silva.

Carlos Gomes	Charles Gomes
prazer	pleasure

em conhecê-lo[1]	to know you ("in knowing you")
Carlos Gomes. Prazer em conhecê-lo.	Charles Gomes. I'm glad to know you.
permita-me	allow me
apresentar-lhe	to introduce to you
(o) meu amigo	my friend
o doutor Sousa	Dr. Sousa
Permita-me apresentar-lhe (o) meu amigo, o doutor Sousa.	I should like to introduce my friend, Dr. Sousa.
muito prazer	much pleasure
em conhecê-lo	to know you
Dr. Sousa	Dr. Sousa
Muito prazer em conhecê-lo, Dr. Sousa.	I'm very glad to know you, Dr. Sousa.
o prazer	the pleasure
é todo meu	is all mine
O prazer é todo meu.	The pleasure is all mine.

20. A GOOD TIME

eu	I
me diverti (diverti-me Ⓟ)	had a good time ("amused myself")
muito	very much
Eu me diverti (diverti-me Ⓟ) muito.	I had a good time.

---

[1] Speaking to a woman it would be *conhecê-la*.

eu também	I also
gostei muito	I liked very much
Eu também gostei muito.	I also enjoyed it very much.
até logo	good-by ("until soon")
até breve	good-by ("until soon")
Até logo.	Good-by.
Até breve.	Good-by.
até amanhã	until tomorrow
boa noite	good evening, or good night
Até amanhã.	See you tomorrow.
Boa noite.	Good night.
até	until
já	soon
Até já.	See you soon.
até	until
a volta	the return
Até a volta.	See you when you get back.
passe	get along
bem	well
Passe bem.	Good-by, or Good luck.

LESSON 9

21. WHAT'S NEW?

(What's New?)

| Como vai, Manuel? | How's it going, Manuel? |
| Bem, e você, João? | Well, and how are you, John? |

mais	more
ou	or
menos	less
Mais ou menos.	So, so.
o que	what
há	is there
de	of
nôvo (novo Ⓟ)	new
O que há de nôvo?	What's new?
nada	nothing
e	and
você	you
que	what
está	are you
fazendo (a fazer Ⓟ)	doing
agora	now
Nada. E você? Que está fazendo (a fazer Ⓟ) agora?	Nothing. And you? What are you doing now?
pouca	little
coisa	thing
nada	nothing
de	of
importância	importance
Pouca coisa. Nada de importância.	Not much. Nothing important.
Até logo.	So long.
Passe bem.	Good luck.

QUIZ 6

1. *Como vai?*	1. Not much.
2. *Até logo.*	2. I should like to introduce my friend to you.
3. *Boa noite.*	3. See you tomorrow.
4. *Que há de nôvo?*	4. What's new?
5. *Pouca coisa.*	5. I'm very glad to know you.
6. *Quero apresentar-lhe (o) meu amigo.*	6. How are you?
7. *Até amanhã.*	7. Good night.
8. *Nôvo*	8. Good luck (Goodby).
9. *Muito prazer em conhecê-lo.*	9. New
10. *Passe bem.*	10. So long.

ANSWERS

1—6; 2—10; 3—7; 4—4; 5—1; 6—2; 7—3; 8—9; 9—5; 10—8.

22. TO BE OR NOT TO BE

Ser and *estar* both mean "to be" in Portuguese. *Ser* tends to be used with characteristic features or qualities and *estar* with more temporary conditions or features. Note examples for particular uses of each verb.

SER

eu sou	I am
(tu és)	you are *(familiar)*

êle, ela, o senhor, etc. **é**	he, she, is, you are
nós somos	we are
(vós sois)	(you are)
êles, elas, os senhores, etc. **são**	They, you, etc. are

ESTAR

eu estou	I am
(tu estás)	you are *(familiar)*
êle (ela, o senhor, etc.**) está**	he (she, you, etc.) is, are
nós estamos	we are
(vós estais)	(you are)
êles (elas, os senhores, etc.**) estão**	they (they, you, etc.) are

SER

Êle é médico.	He is a doctor.
Êle é brasileiro.	He is a Brazilian.
Ela é jovem.	She is young.
Êles são inteligentes.	They are intelligent.
É êle.	It is he.
Donde (de onde) é o senhor?	Where are you from?
Sou dos Estados Unidos.	I'm from the United States.
De quem é?	Whose is it?
Isto é dêle.[1]	This is his.
É de madeira?	Is it made of wood?
É tarde.	It is late.
É cedo.	It is early.
É uma hora.	It is one o'clock.

---

[1] **dele** Ⓟ.

São duas.	It is two o'clock.
É preciso.	It is necessary.
A sala é pequena.	The room is small.
O livro é interessante.	The book is interesting.
Nós somos alunos.	We are students.

ESTAR

Onde está (o) meu irmão?	Where is my brother?
Êle está em casa.	He is home.
Estou cansado.	I'm tired.
Estamos prontos.	We are ready.
O café está frio.	The coffee is cold.
As janelas estão abertas.	The windows are open.

QUIZ 7

1. Êle é inteligente.	1. Whose is it?
2. É preciso.	2. Where are you from?
3. Êle é médico.	3. They are Brazilians.
4. Sou aluno.	4. He is a doctor.
5. É uma hora.	5. It's early.
6. Nós somos médicos.	6. It is two o'clock.
7. É de madeira.	7. He is intelligent.
8. Donde é o senhor?	8. It is necessary.
9. Êles estão em casa.	9. I am a student.
10. É cedo.	10. It is one o'clock.
11. Estou cansado.	11. It's made of wood.
12. Êles são brasileiros.	12. We are doctors.
13. De quem é?	13. They are home.
14. É tarde.	14. I'm tired.
15. São duas.	15. It's late.

ANSWERS

1—7; 2—8; 3—4; 4—9; 5—10; 6—12; 7—11; 8—2;
9—13; 10—5; 11—14; 12—3; 13—1; 14—15; 15—6.

23. IT IS

É...	It is ...
É verdade.	It's true.
Não é verdade.	It's not true.
Está...[1]	It is ...
Está certo!	Fine!
Está bem.	All right.
É muito mau.	It's very bad.
É grande.	It's big.
É pequeno.	It's small.
Está caro.	It's expensive.
Está barato.	It's cheap.
É perto.	It's near.
É longe.	It's far.
É difícil.	It's difficult.
É fácil.	It's easy.
É pouco.	It's little. It's not much.
É muito pouco.	It's very little.
É muito.	It's a lot.
É bastante.	It's enough.
Não é bastante.	It's not enough.
Está aqui.	It's here.
Está ali.	It's over there.
É seu.	It's yours (his, etc.)
É meu.	It's mine.
É nosso.	It's ours.
É para o senhor.	It's for you.

---

[1]For the difference between *é* and *está* see section 22 above, and also section 39 of the grammar summary.

QUIZ 8

1. *É muito.*		1. It's enough.
2. *É fácil.*		2. It's not true.
3. *É perto.*		3. It's very bad.
4. *É bastante.*		4. It's near.
5. *Não é verdade.*		5. It's mine.
6. *É muito mau.*		6. It's true.
7. *É pequeno.*		7. It's here.
8. *É verdade.*		8. It's small.
9. *É meu.*		9. It's easy.
10. *Está aqui.*		10. It's a lot.

ANSWERS

1—10; 2—9; 3—4; 4—1; 5—2; 6—3; 7—8; 8—6; 9—5; 10—7.

LESSON 10

24. TO HAVE AND HAVE NOT

(I Know Only a Little Portuguese)

TO HAVE

eu tenho	I have
(tu tens)	you have *(familiar)*
êle tem	he has
nós temos	we have
(vós tendes)	(you have)
êles têm	they have

NOT TO HAVE

eu não tenho	I don't have
(tu não tens)	you don't have *(familiar)*

êle não tem	he doesn't have
nós não temos	we don't have
(vós não tendes)	(you don't have)
êles não têm	they don't have

Tenho tempo.	I have time.
Não tenho tempo.	I don't have time.
Não tenho amigos.	I don't have any friends.
Tenho fome. (Estou com fome.)[1]	I am hungry. ("I have hunger. I am with hunger.")
Temos sêde.[2] **(Estamos com sêde.)**	We are thirsty. ("We have thirst," etc.)
Êle tem frio. (Êle está com frio.)	He is cold.
Êles têm calor. (Êles estão com calor).	They are warm.
O senhor tem razão.	You are right.

25. I KNOW ONLY A LITTLE PORTUGUESE

O senhor fala português?	Do you speak Portuguese?
Falo um pouco.	I speak a little.
Muito pouco.	Very little.
Não muito bem.	Not very well.
Falo português.	I speak Portuguese.
Falo (-o) mal.	I speak (it) poorly.

---

[1] The first form, *Tenho fome,* etc., is more common in Portugal; the second form given, *Estou com fome,* etc., is more common in Brazil.

[2] sede Ⓟ.

Não o falo muito bem.	I don't speak it very well.
Só sei umas poucas palavras (palavras poucas).	I know only a few words.
Não posso dizer muita coisa em português.	I can't say much in Portuguese.
O seu amigo fala português?	Does your friend speak Portuguese?
Não, (o) meu amigo não fala português.	No, my friend doesn't speak Portuguese.
O senhor compreende português?	Do you understand Portuguese?
Compreendo.	I understand (it).
Compreendo tudo mas não falo.	I understand everything but I don't speak (it).
Leio mas não falo.	I read (it) but I don't speak (it).
Não, não compreendo português.	No, I don't understand Portuguese.
Não compreendo português muito bem.	I don't understand Portuguese very well.
Não o pronuncio muito bem.	I don't pronounce it very well.
Preciso de prática.	I need practice.
O senhor me compreende (compreende-me Ⓟ)?	Do you understand me?
Compreendo.	I understand.
Não compreendo muito bem.	I don't understand very well.
Que disse o senhor?	What did you say?
O senhor fala muito depressa.	You speak too fast. You're speaking too fast.

Fale mais devagar.	Speak more slowly.
Tenha a bondade de falar mais devagar.	Please speak more slowly. ("Have the kindness to . . .")
Desculpe, mas não compreendi nada.	Excuse (me), but I didn't understand anything.
Queira repetir.	Please repeat.
Compreende agora?	Do you understand now?
Sim, compreendo.	Yes, I understand.
Que quer dizer isso em português?	What does that mean in Portuguese?
Como se diz "Thanks" em português?	How do you say "Thanks" in Portuguese?
Como se escreve essa palavra?	How do you spell ("write") that word?
Faça o favor de escrevê-la.	Please write it.

LESSON 11

26. DO YOU SPEAK PORTUGUESE?

(Do you speak Portuguese?)

Bom dia, senhor.	Good morning, sir.
Bom dia.	Good morning.
O senhor fala português?	Do you speak Portuguese?
Sim, falo.	Yes, I do. ("I speak")
Não falo inglês.	I don't speak English.

O senhor é português?	Are you Portuguese?
Não senhor, sou brasileiro. Mas tenho um amigo que é português.	No sir, I'm (a) Brazilian. But I have a friend who is Portuguese.
Há quanto tempo o senhor está nos Estados Unidos?	How long have you been in the United States?
Três meses.	Three months.
O senhor vai aprender inglês em pouco tempo. Não é muito difícil.	You'll soon learn English. ("You'll learn English in little time.") It's not very difficult.
Eu acho que é mais difícil do que o senhor diz.	I think it's more difficult than you say.
Talvez o senhor tenha razão. É mais fácil para nós aprender português que para os senhores aprender inglês.	Perhaps you are right. ("Perhaps you have reason.") It is easier for us to learn Portuguese than for you *(pl.)* to learn English.
O senhor fala muito bem português.	You speak Portuguese very well.
Morei vários anos no Brasil.	I lived several years in Brazil.
O senhor tem uma boa pronúncia.	You have a good pronunciation.
Muito obrigado. Mas preciso de praticar.	Thank you. But I need to practice.
Com licença. O avião vai sair.	If you'll excuse me. ("With permission.") The plane is about to leave.

Boa sorte e boa viagem.	Good luck and a pleasant trip.
Adeus.	Good-by.
Adeus.	Good-by.

QUIZ 9

1. Compreendo mas não falo.	1. Do you speak Portuguese?
2. Compreende agora?	2. I need to practice.
3. Não falo muito bem.	3. a little
4. O senhor fala muito depressa.	4. What did you say?
5. Como se escreve essa palavra?	5. Please repeat (it).
6. O senhor fala português?	6. not very well
7. Preciso de praticar.	7. I didn't understand (it) very well.
8. um pouco	8. I understand (it) but I don't speak (it).
9. Faça o favor de repetir.	9. Speak more slowly.
10. não muito bem	10. I don't speak (it) very well.
11. Fale mais devagar.	11. How do you say "Thanks" in Portuguese?
12. Falo (-o) mal.	12. You speak too fast.
13. Que disse o senhor?	13. Do you understand now?
14. Como se diz "Thanks" em português?	14. How do you spell that word?
15. Não compreendi muito bem.	15. I speak (it) poorly.

ANSWERS

1—8; 2—13; 3—10; 4—12; 5—14; 6—1; 7—2; 8—3;
9—5; 10—6; 11—9; 12—15; 13—4; 14—11; 15—7.

27. EXCUSE ME

Desculpe.	Excuse me. (asking pardon for something done)
Com licença.	Excuse me. (asking permission to do something, as to leave, etc.)
Faça o favor de repetir.	Please repeat. ("Do the favor to repeat.")
Com muito prazer.	Gladly. ("With much pleasure.")
Às suas ordens.	At your service. ("At your orders.")
Em que posso servi-lo?	What can I do for you? ("In what can I serve you?")
O senhor é muito amável.	You are very kind. That's very kind of you.
Obrigado.	Thank you.
Muito obrigado.	Many thanks.
Muitíssimo obrigado.	Many, many thanks.
De nada.	Don't mention it.
Não há de quê.	Don't mention it.
Não é nada.	It's nothing.
Não foi nada.	Don't mention it. ("It wasn't anything.")

Dá licença?   May I ("Do you give
                    permission?")
Pois não.   Of course.

LESSON 12

28. THIS AND THAT

(This and That)

Dê-me êste.[1]	Give me this one. *(masc.)*
Dê-me esta.	Give me this one. *(fem.)*
Dê-me êstes.[1]	Give me these. *(masc.)*
Dê-me estas.	Give me these. *(fem.)*
Dê-me êsse.[1]	Give me that one. *(masc.)* (near the person spoken to; also in next three examples)
Dê-me essa.	Give me that one. *(fem.)*
Dê-me êsses.[1]	Give me those. *(masc.)*
Dê-me essas.	Give me those. *(fem.)*
Dê-me aquêle.[1]	Give me that one. *(masc.)* (something farther away; also in the next three examples)
Dê-me aquela.	Give me that one. *(fem.)*
Dê-me aquêles.[1]	Give me those. *(masc.)*
Dê-me aquelas.	Give me those. *(fem.)*
Fico com êste.	I'll take this one.
Fico com êstes, *etc.*	I'll take these, etc.

---

[1] este, estes, esse, esses, aquele, aqueles Ⓟ.

These forms are also used before nouns:

êste menino	this boy
esta senhora	this lady
essa bandeira	that flag (near you)
aquêle rapaz	that young boy (over there)
aquêles vizinhos	those neighbors

QUIZ 10

1. *Dê-me êstes.*	1. Give me those over there.
2. *Êste.*	2. That one over there.
3. *Dê-me essa.*	3. This lady.
4. *Êste menino.*	4. This one.
5. *Êsse.*	5. That young boy over there.
6. *Aquêles vizinhos.*	6. This boy.
7. *Dê-me aquêles.*	7. Give me these.
8. *Aquêle.*	8. That one (near you).
9. *Esta senhora.*	9. Those neighbors.
10. *Aquêle rapaz.*	10. Give me that one. *(fem.)*

ANSWERS

1—7; 2—4; 3—10; 4—6; 5—8; 6—9; 7—1; 8—2; 9—3; 10—5.

29. MORE OR LESS

1. More

mais devagar	more slowly
mais difícil	more difficult

mais fácil	easier
mais longe	farther
mais perto	nearer
mais que isso	more than that
mais dum ano	more than a year

2. Less

menos devagar	less slowly
menos difícil	less difficult
menos fácil	less easy
menos longe	less far, not so far
menos perto	not so near
menos que isso	less than that
menos dum ano	less than a year

REVIEW QUIZ 2

1. _____ (this) *menino.*
   - a. esta
   - b. êste
   - c. essa

2. *Dê-me* _____ (those, *fem.*).
   - a. essas
   - b. êstes
   - c. aquêle

3. *Tenho* _____ (here) *os livros.*
   - a. isso
   - b. aqui
   - c. como

4. *O senhor fala muito* ____ (fast).
   a. *devagar*
   b. *bem*
   c. *depressa*

5. *Amanhã vou* ____ (there).
   a. *lá*
   b. *aqui*
   c. *êsse*

6. ____ (where) *está?*
   a. *aqui*
   b. *onde*
   c. *como*

7. *É* ____ (far) *daqui.*
   a. *longe*
   b. *perto*
   c. *ali*

8. *Hoje é* ____ (Friday).
   a. *quinta-feira*
   b. *sexta-feira*
   c. *fevereiro*

9. *É muito* ____ (expensive).
   a. *caro*
   b. *barato*
   c. *pouco*

10. *As janelas estão* ____ (open).
    a. *fechadas*
    b. *abertas*
    c. *ali*

ANSWERS

1 b.; 2 a.; 3 b.; 4 c.; 5 a.; 6 b.; 7 a.; 8 b.; 9 a.; 10 b.

30. "AND" AND "BUT"

1. *e* "and"

O Roberto e o João são irmãos.	Robert and John are brothers.

2. *ou* "or"

Cinco ou seis dólares.	Five or six dollars.
Vou com (o) meu irmão ou com (a) minha irmã.	I'm going with my brother or with my sister.

3. *mas* "but"

Quero ir mas não sei quando.	I want to go but I don't know when.
Desejo estudar mas não posso.	I want to study but I can't.

4. *nem* "nor" "not even"

Nem (o) meu cunhado me visitou.	Not even my brother-in-law visited me.

nem . . . nem "neither . . . nor"

Nem o soldado nem o marinheiro vieram.	Neither the soldier nor the sailor came.
Ela nem riu nem chorou.	She neither laughed nor cried.

QUIZ 11

1. *inglês*	1. five or six days
2. *e*	2. He is not French but English.
3. *mas*	3. seven or eight hours
4. *cunhado*	4. English
5. *irmão*	5. but
6. *cinco ou seis dias*	6. tomorrow
7. *quando*	7. brother-in-law
8. *Êle não é francês mas inglês.*	8. and
9. *amanhã*	9. when
10. *sete ou oito horas*	10. brother

ANSWERS

1—4; 2—8; 3—5; 4—7; 5—10; 6—1; 7—9; 8—2;
9—6; 10—3.

LESSON 13

31. WHERE?

(Where?)

1. Where?

Onde está?	Where is it?
Aqui.	Here.
Ali.	There.
À direita.	To the right.
À esquerda.	To the left.
Na esquina.	On the corner.

Fica na Rua da Liberdade.	It's on Liberty Street.
Fica na Praça de Santa Ana.	It's on Saint Anne's Square.
Por onde?	Which way?
Por aqui.	This way.
Por ali.	That way.
Como se vai lá?	How do you get there?
Siga bem em frente.	Continue straight ahead.
Dobre (vire Ⓟ) à direita.	Turn to your right.
Dobre (vire Ⓟ) à esquerda.	Turn to your left.
Onde é isso?	Where's that?
É aqui.	It's here.
É aqui mesmo.	It's right here.
É ali.	It's there.
É mais adiante.	It's farther on.
É longe?	Is it far?
A que distância fica?	How far is it from here?
Fica (é) perto.	It's near.
Não é muito longe.	It's not very far.
É longe daqui?	Is it far from here?
Onde estão os óculos?	Where are the eyeglasses?
Estão aqui.	They are here.
Estão aqui mesmo.	They are right here.
Estão ali.	They're over there (away from us).
Estão aí.	They're there (near you).
Onde está o senhor?	Where are you?
Estou aqui.	Here I am.
Êle está aqui.	He's here.
Ela está ali.	She's over there.

Êles estão por aí.	They're over there somewhere.
Ponha-o aqui.	Put it here.
Ponha-o ali.	Put it there.
Espere-me aqui.	Wait for me here.
Espere-me aí.	Wait for me there.
Venha cá.	Come over here.
Vá lá.	Go over there.
Lá muito longe.	Way over there.
Aqui perto.	Near here.

LESSON 14

(Aqui e Ali)	*(Here and There)*
Lá na África.	Over there in Africa.
Aqui na América.	Here in America.
Lá dentro.	In there.
Lá fora.	Out there.
Onde (êle) mora?	Where does he live?
Mora ali.	He lives there.
Espero vê-lo ali.	I expect to see him there.
Ela está ali.	She is there.
(O) João mora aqui?	Does John live here?
Mora.	He does.
Não, não mora aqui. **Mora ali.**	No, he doesn't live here. He lives there.
Passe por aqui.	Go this way.
Passe por ali.	Go that way.
Saia por ali.	Go out that way.

2. Here and There

Aqui "here" refers to something near the speaker:

Tenho aqui os sapatos.　　　I have the shoes here.

Aí "there" refers to something near the person spoken to:

(O) que tem (o senhor) aí?　　　What do you have there?

Cá "here" expresses motion toward the speaker:

Venha cá!　　　Come here!

Ali "there" refers to something away from both:

Êles vêm dáli.　　　They're coming from over there.

Lá "there" refers to something more remote:

Êle ficou lá no norte.　　　He stayed there in the north.

(*Acolá* is used in some areas).

Note: *Por aqui* means "this way" or "through here"; *por ali* means "that way" or "through there":

Passe por aqui.　　　Go this way.

3. Near and Far

Perto daqui.	Near here.
Muito perto.	Very near.
Perto da cidade.	Near the city.
Perto do parque.	Near the park.
Ao lado da igreja.	Next to the church.
É longe?	Is it far?
É longe daqui?	Is it far from here?
É muito longe.	It is very far.
Não é tão longe.	It's not very far.

Fica a duas quadras Ⓑ **(dois quarteirões) daqui.**	It's two blocks from here.
Fica a uma milha daqui.	It's a mile from here.
Fica a mil quilômetros[1] daqui.	It's a thousand kilometers from here.

QUIZ 12

1. *Lá na África.*	1. I expect to see him there.
2. *Espere-me aí.*	2. In there.
3. *Aqui.*	3. To the left.
4. *À direita.*	4. It's far.
5. *Ali.*	5. Here.
6. *É aqui mesmo.*	6. Wait for me there.
7. *Espero vê-lo ali.*	7. Near here.
8. *À esquerda.*	8. To the right.
9. *É longe.*	9. There.
10. *Lá dentro.*	10. Out there.
11. *Êle está por aí.*	11. Go that way.
12. *É perto.*	12. It's right here.
13. *Lá fora.*	13. Over there in Africa.
14. *Passe por ali.*	14. He's somewhere around there.
15. *Perto daqui.*	15. It's near.

ANSWERS

1—13; 2—6; 3—5; 4—8; 5—9; 6—12; 7—1; 8—3; 9—4; 10—2; 11—14; 12—15; 13—10; 14—11; 15—7.

---

[1] **quilómetros** Ⓟ.

32. I, YOU, HE

1. I, You, He, etc.

SINGULAR

eu	I
(tu)	(you) *(familiar)*
êle	he
ela	she
o senhor	you *(masc., polite)*
a senhora	you *(fem., polite)*
você	you *(friendly)*
eu falo	I speak
(tu falas)	(you speak) *(familiar)*
êle fala	he speaks
ela fala	she speaks
o senhor fala	you speak *(masc.)*
a senhora fala	you speak *(fem.)*
você fala	you speak

PLURAL

nós	we
(vós)	(you)
êles	they *(masc.)*
elas	they *(fem.)*
os senhores	you *(masc.)*
as senhoras	you *(fem.)*
vocês	you
nós falamos	we speak
(vós falais)	(you speak)
êles falam	they speak *(masc.)*
elas falam	they speak *(fem.)*
os senhores falam	you speak *(masc.)*
as senhoras falam	you speak *(fem.)*
vocês falam	you speak

2. It's Me (I)

Sou eu.	It's me (I).
(És tu.)	(It's you.) *(familiar)*
É êle.	It's he.
É ela.	It's she.
É o senhor.	It's you. *(masc.)*
É a senhora.	It's you. *(fem.)*
É você.	It's you.
Somos nós.	It's us (we).
(Sois vós.)	(It's you.)
São êles.	It's them (they) *(masc.)*
São elas.	It's them (they) *(fem.)*

3. My, Your, His

The possessive adjectives and pronouns will agree with the word they refer to in gender *(masc.* or *fem.)* and number *(sing.* or *plural).* This accounts for the four forms for each:

Masc. Sing.	*Fem. Sing.*	*Masc. Pl.*	*Fem. Pl.*	
meu	*minha*	*meus*	*minhas*	my
(teu	*tua*	*teus*	*tuas)*	your *(familiar)*
seu	*sua*	*seus*	*suas*	your (his, her)
nosso	*nossa*	*nossos*	*nossas*	our
(vosso	*vossa*	*vossos*	*vossas)*	your
seu	*sua*	*seus*	*suas*	your (their)

LESSON 15

(Useful Word Forms)

Study the following examples:

SINGULAR

meu amigo	my friend *(masc.)*
minha amiga	my friend *(fem.)*
(teu amigo)	(your friend) *(familiar)*
(tua amiga)	(your friend) *(familiar)*
seu amigo	your (his, her) friend
sua amiga	your (his, her) friend
nosso amigo	our friend
nossa amiga	our friend
(vosso amigo)	(your friend)
(vossa amiga)	(your friend)
seu amigo	your friend (their friend)
sua amiga	your friend (their friend)

PLURAL

meus amigos	my friends
minhas amigas	my friends
(teus amigos)	(your friends) *(familiar)*
(tuas amigas)	(your friends) *(familiar)*
seus amigos	your (his, her) friends
suas amigas	your (his, her) friends
nossos amigos	our friends
nossas amigas	our friends
(vossos amigos)	(your friends)
(vossas amigas)	(your friends)
seus amigos	your friends (their friends)
suas amigas	your friends (their friends)

SINGULAR

meu relógio	my watch
minha sobrinha	my niece
seu sobrinho	your (his, her) nephew
sua prima	your (his, her) cousin *(fem.)*
nosso primo	our cousin *(masc.)*
nossa sogra	our mother-in-law
seu sogro	your (their) father-in-law
sua tia	your (their) aunt

PLURAL

meus relógios	my watches
minhas sobrinhas	my nieces
seus sobrinhos	your (his, her) nephews
suas primas	your (his, her) cousins
nossos primos	our cousins
nossas sogras	our mothers-in-law
seus sogros	your (their) fathers-in-law
suas tias	your (their) aunts

Other Examples:

MASCULINE SINGULAR

Onde está (o) meu irmão? [1]	Where is my brother?
Onde está (o) seu irmão?	Where is your (his, her) brother?

---

[1] The use of the definite article with possessive adjectives is optional. However, the tendency is to use the article, more so in Portugal than in Brazil (where it is often not used with family or other close relationships: *meu pai* my father, *minha irmã* my sister, etc.): *o meu amigo, a minha amiga,* etc.

Onde está (o) nosso irmão?	Where is our brother?
Onde está (o) seu irmão?	Where is your (their) brother?

FEMININE SINGULAR

Onde está (a) minha irmã?	Where is my sister?
Onde está (a) sua irmã?	Where is your (his, her) sister?
Onde está (a) nossa irmã?	Where is our sister?
Onde está (a) sua irmã?	Where is your (their) sister?

MASCULINE PLURAL

Onde estão (os) meus chapéus?	Where are my hats?
Onde estão (os) seus chapéus?	Where are your (his, her) hats?
Onde estão (os) nossos chapéus?	Where are our hats?
Onde estão (os) seus chapéus?	Where are your (their) hats?

FEMININE PLURAL

Onde estão (as) minhas luvas?	Where are my gloves?
Onde estão (as) suas luvas?	Where are your (his, her) gloves?
Onde estão (as) nossas luvas?	Where are our gloves?
Onde estão (as) suas luvas?	Where are your (their) gloves?

4. It's Mine

There are two forms, one without the definite article and stressing the possessor:

a. **É meu.**   It's mine.
   É seu.   It's yours (his, hers).

   É nosso.   It's ours.
   É seu.   It's yours (theirs).

b. and one with the definite article, indicating the possessor, but with some thought on the object possessed:

   É o meu.   It's mine.
   É o seu.   It's yours (his, hers).

   É o nosso.   It's ours.
   É o seu.   It's yours (theirs).

Other Examples:

Meus amigos e os seus.	My friends and yours.
Seu livro é melhor que o nosso.	Your book is better than ours.
De quem é a luva?—É minha.	Whose glove is this?— It's mine.

Notice the form of the pronoun when it comes after a preposition:

SINGULAR

para mim	for me
(para ti)	(for you) *(familiar)*
para êle	for him
com ela	with her

sem o senhor	without you *(masc.)*
de você	of you

PLURAL

por nós	for us (in our behalf)
(para vós)	(for you)
com êles	with them *(masc.)*
sem elas	without them *(fem.)*
para as senhoras	for you *(fem.)*
com vocês	with you

5. He Saw Me

Êle me viu.[1]	He saw me.
(Êle te viu.)	(He saw you.) *(familiar)*
Êle o viu.	He saw him (you, *masc.*).
Êle a viu.	He saw her (you, *fem.*).
Êles nos viram.	They saw us.
(Êles vos viram.)	(They saw you.)
Nós os vimos.	We saw them (you, *masc.*).

---

[1] In Continental Portuguese:
> **Ele viu-me.**
> **(Ele viu-te.)**
> **Ele viu-o.**
> **Ele viu-a.**
> **Eles viram-nos.**
> **(Eles viram-vos.)**
> **Nós vimo-los.** (See item 5, section
> **Nós vimo-las.** 20, grammar summary.)

Brazilian usage favors the object pronoun before the verb, Continental Portuguese favors it after the verb. For more information on the position of object pronouns see section 20 of the grammar summary.

Nós as vimos.	We saw them (you, *fem.*).

6. About Me

Falo de você.	I'm speaking about you.
(Falas de mim.)	(You [*familiar*] are speaking about me.)
Ela fala dêle.	She is speaking about him.
Êle fala dela.	He is speaking about her.
Falamos dos senhores.	We are speaking about you *(masc.)*.
(Falais de nós.)	(You are speaking about us.)
Êles falam das senhoras.	They *(masc.)* are speaking about you *(fem.)*
Elas falam dêles.	They *(fem.)* are speaking about them *(masc.)*.

7. He Told Me

Êle me disse.[1]	He told me.
(Êle te disse.)	(He told you.) *(familiar)*
Êle lhe disse.	He told you, him, her.
Êle nos disse.	He told us.
(Êle vos disse.)	(He told you.)
Êle lhes disse.	He told you, them.

[1] In the examples in section 7, 8, 9 and 10 on pp. 71–73, Continental Portuguese would favor the object pronoun after the verb: *Ele disse-me, Ele deu-me*, etc.

Note: It is generally not considered the best form to begin a sentence or a clause with an object pronoun. The subject pronoun may precede, as above, or the object pronoun may follow the verb and be attached to it with a hyphen: *Disse-me.* However, in Brazilian speech this has become quite common and must be considered an acceptable pattern.

8. He Gave It to Me

Êle me deu.	He gave it to me.
(Êle te deu.)	(He gave it to you.) *(familiar)*
Êle lhe deu.	He gave it to you, him, her.
Êle nos deu.	He gave it to us.
(Êle vos deu.)	(He gave it to you.)
Êle lhes deu.	He gave it to you, them.

Note: The direct object pronoun, if used with an indirect object pronoun, is contracted with it, forming such new forms as *mo, to, lho, no-lo, vo-lo,* and *lho.* These forms are somewhat awkward and are generally avoided, especially in conversation. Thus, the direct object pronoun may be omitted, as in the examples above, or the direct object pronoun may be used and the indirect object replaced by the prepositional form: *Êle o deu a mim,* etc.

9. I'm Speaking to You

Eu lhe falo, or, *Falo-lhe.*	I'm speaking to you.

Êle lhe fala, or, *Fala-lhe.*	He is speaking to you.

10. Myself, Yourself

Eu me lavo.	I wash myself.
(Tu te lavas.)	(You wash yourself.) *(familiar)*
Êle, ela, o senhor, você se lava.	He washes himself, she washes herself, you wash yourself.
Nós nos lavamos.	We wash ourselves.
(Vós vos lavais.)	(You wash yourselves.)
Êles se lavam.	They wash themselves.
Elas se lavam, etc.	They *(fem.)* wash themselves, etc.

Other Examples:

Como se chama o senhor?	What is your name? ("What do you call yourself?")
Nós nos vemos no espelho.	We see ourselves in the mirror.
Êles se escrevem.	They write to each other.

Notice the forms for "myself," "yourself," etc.: *me, te, se,* etc. Verbs which take these "reflexive pronouns" are called "reflexive" verbs. There are verbs which are reflexive in Portuguese but not in English as, for example:

Eu me divirto.	I'm having a good time.
Êle se senta.	He sits down.
Nós nos levantamos.	We get up. We are getting up.
Ela não se sente bem.	She doesn't feel well.

Some of these reflexive verbs use a preposition before a following object:

Êles se despedem de seus amigos.	They are taking leave of their friends.
Ela se ri de nós.	She is laughing at us.
O senhor não se atreve a dizer-me.	You don't dare tell me.

The "*se*" form is often used where the passive form would be used in English:

Fala-se português aqui.	Portuguese is spoken here.
As portas se abrem às oito.	The doors are opened at eight.

The "*se*" form is also used to translate the indefinite "one," "they," "people," etc., in English:

Diz-se que...	It's said that ... They say that ... People say that ...
Aprende-se muito aqui.	You ("one learns") learn a lot here.

QUIZ 13

1. *Senta-se.*	1. We get up.
2. *Nós nos vemos.*	2. They are taking leave.
3. *Divirto-me.*	3. He gave it to them.
4. *Disse-me.*	4. She laughs.
5. *Nós nos levantamos.*	5. I wash myself.
6. *Eu me lavo.*	6. I'm having a good time.
7. *Ri-se.*	7. They write to each other.

8. *Escrevem-se.*	8. He told me.
9. *Deu-lhes.*	9. We see ourselves.
10. *Despedem-se.*	10. He sits down.

ANSWERS

1—10; 2—9; 3—6; 4—8; 5—1; 6—5; 7—4; 8—7;
9—3; 10—2.

11. It and Them

SINGULAR		PLURAL	
Masculine	*o* it	*os*	them
Feminine	*a* it	*as*	them

O senhor tem o dinheiro?	Do you have the money?
Tenho. (Sim, tenho-o.)	Yes, I have it.
O senhor tem a carta?	Do you have the letter?
Tenho. (Sim, tenho-a.)	Yes, I have it.
O senhor viu João e Pedro?	Did you see John and Peter?
Vi. (Sim, vi-os.)	Yes, I saw them.
O senhor viu Maria e Ana?	Did you see Mary and Anna?
Vi. (Sim, vi-as.)	Yes, I saw them.

Notice that the pronoun is masculine if the word
it refers to is masculine, plural if the word it refers
to is plural, etc. In conversation a short answer is
often given, as just the verb form as shown above.
If the object pronoun is used in the answer, it can
follow the verb, as shown above in parentheses,
or it can precede the verb: *Sim, eu os tenho,* etc.

Generally an object pronoun used with an infinitive may precede or follow the infinitive if a preposition comes before the infinitive (however, with the prepositions *a* and *em* the pronoun comes after the infinitive):

para me falar or *para falar-me*	to speak to me

In the above case, and when the infinitive follows another verb, Brazilian usage usually favors using the object pronoun before the infinitive:

Êle quer me falar.	He wants to speak to me.

Notice that *o, os, a, as,* are also used to translate "you":

Não o vi.	I didn't see you. (*masc. sing.*)
Muito prazer em conhecê-la.	I'm very glad to know you. (*fem. sing.*)
Êle os chamou.	He called you. (*masc. pl.*)

Notice in the second example above that when a direct object pronoun follows the infinitive, the final *r* of the infinitive is dropped and an *l* is prefixed to the direct object pronoun.

REVIEW QUIZ 3

1. *É* _____ (she).
   a. *êle*
   b. *ela*
   c. *eu*

2. *Somos* ____ (us).
   a. *êles*
   b. *tu*
   c. *nós*

3. *Dou o livro a* ____ (him).
   a. *êle*
   b. *o senhor*
   c. *o*

4. ____ (her) *vestido.*
   a. *(o) seu*
   b. *(o) meu*
   c. *(o) nosso*

5. ____ (our) *cartas.*
   a. *(o) nosso*
   b. *(as) nossas*
   c. *(o) teu*

6. *Onde estão* ____ (my) *livros?*
   a. *(os) teus*
   b. *(os) meus*
   c. *(a) nossa*

7. *Seu livro é melhor que o* ____ (ours).
   a. *vossos*
   b. *nosso*
   c. *seu*

8. *Falamos* ____ (about him).
   a. *o senhor*
   b. *dêles*
   c. *dêle*

9. *Êle* _____ (us) *deu.*
   a. *se*
   b. *nos*
   c. *nossos*

10. *Como se* _____ (call) *o senhor?*
    a. *lavo*
    b. *chama*
    c. *vemos*

11. *Nós nos* _____ (wash).
    a. *lava*
    b. *lavais*
    c. *lavamos*

12. _____ -*se* (They take leave).
    a. *despedem*
    b. *levantam*
    c. *sente*

13. _____ -*me* (sit down).
    a. *diz*
    b. *lavo*
    c. *sento*

14. *Falo-* _____ (to him).
    a. *a êles*
    b. *o senhor*
    c. *lhe*

15. *Não se* _____ (dare).
    a. *atreve*
    b. *lavam*
    c. *levantamos*

ANSWERS

1 b.; 2 c.; 3 a.; 4 a.; 5 b.; 6 b.; 7 b.; 8 c.; 9 b.; 10 b.;
11 c.; 12 a.; 13 c.; 14 c.; 15 a.

LESSON 16

33. A FEW SHORT PHRASES

(Useful Phrases)

Cuidado!	Watch out
Tenha cuidado!	Be careful! Watch out!
Atenção!	Attention! Watch out!
Depressa!	Hurry up!
Mais depressa.	Faster.
Devagar.	Slowly.
Mais devagar.	Slower.
Já vou.	I'm coming.
Vamos embora.	Let's leave.
Vamos lá.	Let's go.
Vamos! Depressa!	Come on, let's hurry!
Não há pressa.	There's no hurry.
Estou com pressa.	I'm in a hurry.
Não estou com pressa.	I'm not in a hurry.
Um momento!	Just a minute!
Venha já!	Come right away!
Imediatamente.	Immediately.
Agora mesmo!	Right now!
Aqui mesmo.	Right here.
Cedo.	Soon.
Mais cedo.	Sooner.
Mais tarde.	Later.
Muito bem. Está certo.	Very well. All right.

QUIZ 14

1. *Cuidado!*	1. Slower.
2. *Estou com pressa.*	2. Right now!
3. *Um momento!*	3. Come right away!
4. *Cedo.*	4. I'm coming.
5. *Imediatamente.*	5. Watch out!
6. *Mais tarde.*	6. Later.
7. *Mais devagar.*	7. I'm in a hurry.
8. *Já vou.*	8. Just a minute!
9. *Venha já!*	9. Immediately.
10. *Agora mesmo!*	10. Soon.

ANSWERS

1—5; 2—7; 3—8; 4—10; 5—9; 6—6; 7—1; 8—4;
9—3; 10—2.

34. MAY I ASK?

Permite que lhe faça uma pergunta?	May I ask you a question?
Permita-me perguntar-lhe ...	Allow me to ask you ...
Pode me dizer (dizer-me Ⓟ)?	Can you tell me?
Podia me dizer (dizer-me Ⓟ)?	Could you tell me?
Queira me dizer (dizer-me Ⓟ).	Please tell me.
Tenha a bondade de me dizer (dizer-me Ⓟ).	Please tell me.
Faça o favor de me dizer (dizer-me Ⓟ).	Please tell me.
Quer me dizer (dizer-me Ⓟ).	Will you tell me?

Que quer dizer o senhor?	What do you mean?
Quero dizer que ...	I mean that ...
Que quer dizer isso?	What does that mean?
Quer dizer ...	It means ...

LESSON 17

35. NUMBERS

1. One, Two, Three

um *(masc.)* **uma** *(fem.)*	one
dois *(masc.)* **duas** *(fem.)*	two
três	three
quatro	four
cinco	five
seis	six
sete	seven
oito	eight
nove	nine
dez	ten
onze	eleven
doze	twelve
treze	thirteen
catorze (quatorze)	fourteen
quinze	fifteen
dezesseis (dezasseis Ⓟ)	sixteen
dezessete (dezassete Ⓟ)	seventeen
dezoito	eighteen
dezenove (dezanove Ⓟ)	nineteen
vinte	twenty
vinte e um *(uma)*	twenty-one
vinte e dois *(duas)*	twenty-two
vinte e três	twenty-three

trinta	thirty
trinta e um *(uma)*	thirty-one
trinta e dois *(duas)*	thirty-two
trinta e três	thirty-three
quarenta	forty
quarenta e um *(uma)*	forty-one
quarenta e dois *(duas)*	forty-two
quarenta e três	forty-three
cinqüenta[1]	fifty
cinqüenta e um *(uma)*	fifty-one
cinqüenta e dois *(duas)*	fifty-two
cinqüenta e três	fifty-three
sessenta	sixty
sessenta e um *(uma)*	sixty-one
sessenta e dois *(duas)*	sixty-two
sessenta e três	sixty-three
setenta	seventy
setenta e um *(uma)*	seventy-one
setenta e dois *(duas)*	seventy-two
setenta e três	seventy-three
oitenta	eighty
oitenta e um *(uma)*	eighty-one
oitenta e dois *(duas)*	eighty-two
oitenta e três	eighty-three
noventa	ninety
noventa e um *(uma)*	ninety-one

---

[1] cinquenta Ⓟ.

noventa e dois *(duas)*	ninety-two
noventa e três	ninety-three
cem	one hundred
cento e um *(uma)*	a hundred and one
cento e dois *(duas)*	a hundred and two
cento e três	a hundred and three
mil	one thousand
mil e um *(uma)*	a thousand and one
mil e dois *(duas)*	a thousand and two
mil e três	a thousand and three

2. **Some More Numbers**

    120 cento e vinte
    122 cento e vinte e dois (duas)
    130 cento e trinta
    140 cento e quarenta
    150 cento e cinqüenta
    160 cento e sessenta
    170 cento e setenta
    178 cento e setenta e oito
    200 duzentos, duzentas
    300 trezentos, trezentas
    400 quatrocentos, quatrocentas
    500 quinhentos, quinhentas
    600 seiscentos, seiscentas
    700 setecentos, setecentas
    800 oitocentos, oitocentas
    900 novecentos, novecentas
    1965 mil novecentos e sessenta e cinco
1,000,000 um milhão (de)

Notice that in addition to the numbers "one" and

"two" the plural hundred forms also have feminine forms: *duzentos, duzentas,* etc. *Milhão* uses *de* before a completing noun: *um milhão de dólares.*

LESSON 18

(How Much?)

3. First, Second, Third

The following ordinal numbers each have four forms, masculine singular and plural, and feminine singular and plural: *primeiro, primeiros, primeira, primeiras,* etc.

primeiro	first
segundo	second
terceiro	third
quarto	fourth
quinto	fifth
sexto	sixth
sétimo	seventh
oitavo	eighth
nono	ninth
décimo	tenth

4. Two and Two

Dois e dois: quatro. Two and two are four.
(Also used: *Dois mais dois são quatro; Dois mais dois igual a quatro.*)
Quatro e dois: seis. Four and two are six.
Dez menos dois: oito. Ten minus two is eight.

Sete vêzes¹ três: vinte   Seven times three is
   e um.   twenty-one.
Oito vêzes oito: sessenta Eight times eight is
   e quatro.   sixty-four.
Vinte e um divido por   Twenty-one divided by
   sete: três.   seven is three.

QUIZ 15

1. mil	1. 1002
2. onze	2. 32
3. cem	3. 102
4. terceiro	4. 324
5. trinta	5. 11
6. vinte	6. 1000
7. sessenta e sete	7. 67
8. trezentos e vinte e	8. 71
* quatro*	
9. trinta e dois	9. 3rd
10. cento e dois	10. 875
11. oitocentos e setenta	11. 83
* e cinco*	
12. setenta e um	12. 555
13. mil e dois	13. 20
14. quinhentos e cinqüenta	14. 30
* e cinco*	
15. oitenta e três	15. 100

ANSWERS

1—6; 2—5; 3—15; 4—9; 5—14; 6—13; 7—7; 8—4;
9—2; 10—3; 11—10; 12—8; 13—1; 14—12; 15—11.

---

¹ **vezes** Ⓟ.

36. HOW MUCH?

Quanto custa isto?	How much does this cost?
Custa quarenta centavos.	It costs forty cents.
Quanto é uma libra (um quilo) de café?	How much is a pound (a kilogram) of coffee?
Estamos vendendo a oitenta centavos a libra (o quilo).	It costs eighty cents a pound (a kilogram). ("We're selling at eighty cents," etc.)

37. IT COSTS . . .

Custa . . .	It costs . . .
Êste livro custa sessenta cruzeiros.	This book costs sixty cruzeiros.
Êle comprou um carro por dois mil dólares.	He bought a car for two thousand dollars.
A viagem de navio é trezentos dólares.	The trip by ship is three hundred dollars.
Tenho economizado para poder comprar um sobretudo.	I've saved to be able to buy an overcoat.
No mês de junho[1] êle ganhou mais de um conto.	In the month of June he earned more than a conto (1000 cruzeiros or escudos).
Vende-se só por (or ao) quilo.	It is sold only by the kilogram.

---

[1] **Junho** Ⓟ.

38. MY ADDRESS IS . . .

Eu moro na Rua do Passeio (no) (número), duzentos e trinta.	I live at 230 Passeio Street.
Ela mora na Praça da Bandeira.	She lives on Bandeira Plaza.
A loja é na Avenida Rio Branco.	The store is on Rio Branco Avenue.

39. MY TELEPHONE NUMBER IS . . .

O número de meu telefone é três, dois, oito, oito.	My telephone number is 3288.
O número de seu telefone é quatro, zero, oito, dois, zero.	Their telephone number is: 4-0820.
Não esqueça o número de meu telefone; é dois, um, zero, cinco.	Don't forget my telephone number: 2105.
Linha, por favor. Vou discar o número.	Line, please. I'm going to dial the number.
O número sete, um, dois, oito, não responde.	Number 7128 does not answer.

40. THE NUMBER IS . . .

O número é . . .	The number is . . .
Meu número é . . .	My number is . . .

Moro no quarto número trinta.	I live in room 30.
O número de meu apartamento é cento e vinte.	My apartment number is 120.
Moro na Quinta Avenida, trezentos e trinta e dois, quinto andar.	I live at 332 Fifth Avenue, fifth floor.

LESSON 19

41. WHAT'S TODAY?

(What's the Date?)

Que dia da semana é hoje?	What day is it today? ("What day of the week is today?")
É segunda-feira.	It's Monday.
A quantos do mês estamos?	What day of the month is it? ("At how many of the month are we?")
Estamos a vinte.	It's the 20th. ("We're at the 20th.")
Estamos a . . .	It's the . . .
um (primeiro) **de maio.**[1]	1st of May.
onze de abril.	11th of April.
quatro de julho.	4th of July.
quinze de setembro.	15th of September.
vinte e um de junho.	21st of June.

---

[1] In Portugal, **Maio,** etc.

vinte e cinco de dezembro.	25th of December.
dezessete (dezassete ℗) de novembro.	17th of November.
treze de fevereiro.	13th of February.
vinte e oito de agôsto.[1]	28th of August.

42. SOME DATES

A América foi descoberta em mil quatrocentos e noventa e dois.	America was discovered in 1492.
Os portuguêses[2] *descobriram o Brasil em mil e quinhentos.*	The Portuguese discovered Brazil in 1500.
O pai dêle faleceu em mil novecentos e sessenta e dois.	His father died in 1962.
Estivemos lá em mil novecentos e quarenta e seis ou quarenta e sete.	We were there in 1946 or 1947.
Que aconteceu em mil novecentos e quarenta e um?	What happened in 1941?
O presidente Roosevelt faleceu em mil novecentos e quarenta e cinco.	President Roosevelt died in 1945.

---

[1] **Agosto** ℗.
[2] **Portuguese** ℗.

QUIZ 16

1. *É segunda-feira.*	1. On the 25th of June.
2. *A quantos do mês estamos?*	2. On the 28th of February.
3. *A primeiro de julho.*	3. On the 13th of August.
4. *Estamos a vinte.*	4. 1605.
5. *A onze de abril.*	5. It's Monday.
6. *A vinte e oito de fevereiro.*	6. What day of the month is it?
7. *A vinte e cinco de junho.*	7. He died.
8. *Mil seiscentos e cinço.*	8. On the 1st of July.
9. *A treze de agôsto.*	9. On the 11th of April.
10. *Faleceu.*	10. It's the 20th.

ANSWERS

1—5; 2—6; 3—8; 4—10; 5—9; 6—2; 7—1; 8—4; 9—3; 10—7.

43. WHAT TIME IS IT?

Que horas são?	What time is it?
É uma hora.	1:00.
É uma e cinco.	1:05.
É uma e dez.	1:10.
É uma e quinze.	1:15.
É uma e um quarto.	1:15.
É uma e meia.	1:30.
Faltam dez para as duas.	1:50 ("ten minutes to two").

São duas (horas).	2:00.
São três.	3:00.
São quatro.	4:00.
São cinco.	5:00.
São seis.	6:00.
São sete.	7:00.
São oito.	8:00.
São nove.	9:00.
São dez horas.	10:00.
São onze.	11:00.
É meio-dia.	12:00. It's noon.
É meia-noite.	12:00. It's midnight.

minuto	minute
hora	hour

A que horas?	(At) what time?
A que horas chegou?	At what time did you arrive?
Por favor, diga-me que horas são.	Please tell me the time.
Que horas tem o senhor?	What time do you have?
Que horas são pelo seu relógio?	What time is it by your watch?

LESSON 20

(What Time Is It?)

São três e dez.	It's 3:10.
São seis e meia.	It's 6:30.
São duas menos um quarto.	It's a quarter to two.

Ainda não são quatro.	It's not four yet.
A que horas sai o trem (comboio Ⓟ)?	What time does the train leave?
Às nove em ponto.	At 9 o'clock sharp.
Quase às nove.	About 9 o'clock.
São dez horas da manhã.	It's 10 a.m.
Às oito e quarenta da noite.	At 8:40 p.m.
Às seis da tarde.	At 6 p.m.
Às dez da noite.	At 10 p.m.

Notice that to indicate "a.m." or "p.m." you add *da manhã, da tarde* or *da noite*.

44. IT'S TIME

Está na hora.	It's time.
Está na hora de fazê-lo.	It's time to do it.
Está na hora de partir.	It's time to leave.
Está na hora de irmos para casa.	It's time for us to go home.
Tenho muito tempo.	I have a lot of time.
Não tenho tempo.	I haven't any time.
Êle está perdendo (a perder Ⓟ) o tempo.	He's wasting his time.
Ela vem de vez em quando.	She comes from time to time.

QUIZ 17

1. *Está na hora de fazê-lo.*	1. She comes from time to time.
2. *Que horas são?*	2. It's 9:00.

3. *É uma.*	3. At what time?
4. *São três.*	4. It's time to do it.
5. *São nove.*	5. It's 2:00.
6. *É meia-noite.*	6. It's 1:00.
7. *A que horas?*	7. I haven't any time.
8. *Não tenho tempo.*	8. It's 3:40 p.m.
9. *É uma e um quarto.*	9. It's noon.
10. *São quatro horas.*	10. It's 3:00.
11. *São duas.*	11. It's 1:05.
12. *Ela vem de vez em quando.*	12. It's 4:00.
13. *É meio-dia.*	13. What time is it?
14. *É uma e cinco.*	14. It's 1:15.
15. *São três e quarenta da tarde.*	15. It's midnight.

ANSWERS

1—4; 2—13; 3—6; 4—10; 5—2; 6—15; 7—3; 8—7; 9—14; 10—12; 11—5; 12—1; 13—9; 14—11; 15—8.

45. PAST, PRESENT AND FUTURE

PASSADO	PRESENTE	FUTURO
ontem	**hoje**	**amanhã**
yesterday	today	tomorrow
ontem de manhã	**esta manhã**	**amanhã de manhã**
yesterday morning	this morning	tomorrow morning

ontem à tarde	hoje à tarde	amanhã à tarde
yesterday afternoon, last evening	this afternoon, this evening	tomorrow afternoon, tomorrow evening

ontem à noite	hoje à noite	amanhã à noite
last night	this evening	tomorrow night

46. MORNING, NOON AND NIGHT

Esta manhã.	This morning.
Ontem de manhã.	Yesterday morning.
Amanhã de manhã.	Tomorrow morning.
Hoje ao meio-dia.	This noon.
Ontem ao meio-dia.	Yesterday noon.
Amanhã ao meio-dia.	Tomorrow noon.
Hoje à tarde.	This evening (afternoon).
Ontem à tarde.	Yesterday evening.
Amanhã à tarde.	Tomorrow evening.
Hoje à noite.	Tonight.
Ontem à noite.	Last night.
Amanhã à noite.	Tomorrow night.

LESSON 21

(Past, Present and Future)

Esta semana.	This week.
A semana passada.	Last week.
A semana que vem.	Next week.

Dentro de duas semanas.	In two weeks.
Há duas semanas.	Two weeks ago.
Êste mês.	This month.
O mês passado.	Last month.
O mês que vem.	Next month.
No próximo mês.	Next month.
Dentro de dois meses.	In two months.
Há dois meses.	Two months ago.
Êste ano.	This year.
O (no) ano passado.	Last year.
O (no) próximo ano.	Next year.
Dentro de dois anos.	In two years.
Há dois anos.	Two years ago.
Há quanto tempo?	How long ago?
Há pouco tempo.	A short time ago.
Há muito tempo.	A long time ago.
Agora.	Now.
Agora mesmo.	Right now.
Por agora.	For the time being.
Neste instante.	At this moment.
Dentro em pouco..	In a little while.
Daqui a pouco.	In a little while.
Quantas vêzes?[1]	How many times?
Uma vez.	Once.
Duas vêzes.	Twice.
Cada vez.	Each time.
Raras vêzes.	Seldom.
Muitas vêzes.	Often.
Algumas vêzes.	Sometimes.
Às vêzes.	Sometimes.

---

[1] **vezes** Ⓟ. Note: variants previously listed will generally not be repeated.

De vez em quando.	From time to time.
Mais uma vez.	Again.
Pela primeira vez.	For the first time.
De manhã cedo.	Early in the morning.
De madrugada.	Very early in the morning.
Ao anoitecer.	In the evening ("at nightfall").
No dia seguinte.	On the following day.
De hoje a quinze dias.	In two weeks.
De hoje a oito dias.	A week from today.
Dentro de uma semana.	In a week.
Na quarta-feira da próxima semana.	Next Wednesday.
Na segunda-feira da semana passada.	Monday a week ago.
No dia cinco dêste mês.	On the fifth of this month.
A cinco do mês passado.	On the fifth of last month.
Em princípios de março.	Early in March.
Em fins de maio.	Late in May.
Aconteceu há oito anos.	It happened eight years ago.

QUIZ 18

1. *Ontem de manhã.*	1. Last year.
2. *Hoje à tarde.*	2. Last night.
3. *Amanhã à tarde.*	3. Today at noon.
4. *Ontem à noite.*	4. Now.
5. *O próximo mês.*	5. In two weeks.
6. *Agora.*	6. In a little while.
7. *A semana passada.*	7. Yesterday morning.

8. *O ano passado.*
9. *Hoje ao meio-dia.*

10. *Dentro em pouco.*
11. *Esta semana.*
12. *Aconteceu há oito anos.*
13. *Em fins de maio.*

14. *Há dois meses.*
15. *De vez em quando.*
16. *Dentro de uma semana.*
17. *Agora mesmo.*
18. *Às vêzes.*

19. *Dentro de duas semanas.*
20. *Cada vez.*

8. Right now.
9. It happened eight years ago.
10. This afternoon.
11. Sometimes.
12. Within a week.

13. Tomorrow afternoon.

14. Next month.
15. Last week.
16. Each time.

17. From time to time.
18. Toward the end of May.

19. This week.

20. Two months ago.

ANSWERS

1—7; 2—10; 3—13; 4—2; 5—14; 6—4; 7—15; 8—1; 9—3; 10—6; 11—19; 12—9; 13—18; 14—20; 15—17; 16—12; 17—8; 18—11; 19—5; 20—16.

REVIEW QUIZ 4

1. *Êle comprou um carro por* _____ (two thousand) *dólares.*

   a. *três mil*
   b. *quatrocentos*
   c. *dois mil*

2. *O número de seu telefone é* ____ (4-0820).
   a. *dois, cinco, zero, sete, nove*
   b. *cinco, zero, oito, nove, zero*
   c. *quatro, zero, oito, dois, zero*

3. ____ (It's time) *de partir.*
   a. *a que horas*
   b. *há muito tempo*
   c. *está na hora*

4. *A quantos do mês estamos* ____ (today)?
   a. *mês*
   b. *hoje*
   c. *tempo*

5. *A* ____ (17) *de dezembro.*
   a. *dezessete (dezassete ℗)*
   b. *vinte e sete*
   c. *quinze*

6. *É* ____ (1:10).
   a. *uma e cinco*
   b. *uma e dez*
   c. *onze*

7. *São* ____ (7:00).
   a. *sete*
   b. *nove*
   c. *seis*

8. *É* ____ (12:00 noon).
   a. *meia-noite*
   b. *meio-dia*
   c. *duas*

9. *Às* ____ (3:40).
   a. *falta um quarto para as três*
   b. *três e quarenta*
   c. *uma e meia*

10. ____ (yesterday) *de manhã.*
    a. *hoje*
    b. *ontem*
    c. *esta*

11. *A* ____ (week) *passada.*
    a. *semana*
    b. *noite*
    c. *amanhã*

12. *Dentro de dois* ____ (months).
    a. *semana*
    b. *dias*
    c. *meses*

13. *Há dois* ____ (years).
    a. *meses*
    b. *anos*
    c. *dias*

14. *Na* ____ (Wednesday) *da próxima semana.*
    a. *segunda-feira*
    b. *sexta-feira*
    c. *quarta-feira*

15. *Em* ____ (end) *de maio.*
    a. *fins*
    b. *princípios*
    c. *primeiros*

ANSWERS

1 c.; 2 c.; 3 c.; 4 b.; 5 a.; 6 b.; 7 a.; 8 b.; 9 b.; 10 b.;
11 a.; 12c.; 13 b.; 14 c.; 15 a.

LESSON 22

47. NO

(Useful Word Groups I)

The word for "not"—*não*—comes before the verb:

Não vejo.	I don't see.
O senhor não vê.	You don't see.

Such negative words as the forms for "nothing," "never," "nobody," etc. may come after the verb, in which case *não* is used before the verb, or they may precede the verb and then *não* is not used:

Êle não diz nada.	He doesn't say anything.
Êles não trabalham nunca.	They never work.
Não vem ninguém.	Nobody is coming.

Or—

Êle nada diz.	He doesn't say anything.
Êles nunca trabalham.	They never work.
Ninguém vem.	Nobody is coming.

Sim, senhor.	Yes, sir.
Não, senhor.	No, sir.
Êle diz que sim.	He says yes.
Êle diz que não.	He says no.

Acho que sim.	I think so.
Está bem.	All right.
Não está bem.	It's not good.
Não é mau.	It's not bad.
Não é isso.	It's not that.
Êle não está aqui.	He's not here.
Aqui está.	Here it is.
Não é muito.	It's not very much.
Não é bastante.	It's not enough.
É bastante.	It's enough.
Não tão depressa.	Not so fast.
Não é nada.	It's nothing.
Isso não é nada.	That's nothing.
Não tem importância.	It's not important.
Não tenho tempo.	I have no time.
Não sei como nem quando.	I don't know how or when.
Não sei onde.	I don't know where.
Não sei nada.	I don't know anything.
Não sei nada disso.	I don't know anything about that.
Não desejo nada.	I don't want anything.
Nada desejo.	I don't want anything.
Não importa.	It doesn't matter.
Não me importa.	It makes no difference to me.
Não me importa nada.	It makes absolutely no difference to me.
Não me diga!	You don't say!
Não tenho nada que dizer.	I've nothing to say.
Isso não quer dizer nada.	That doesn't mean anything.
Não aconteceu nada.	Nothing happened.

Não diga a ninguém.	Don't tell anybody.
Nunca o vejo.	I never see him.
Nunca o vi.	I never saw him.
Êle nunca vem.	He never comes.
Êle nunca veio.	He never came.
Nunca vou.	I never go.
Nunca irei.	I'll never go.

LESSON 23

(Useful Word Groups II)

Nem.
Nor.

Eu não disse (nem) sequer uma palavra.
I didn't say a word.

Nem ... nem ...
Neither ... nor ...

Nem mais nem menos.
Just so ("neither more nor less").

Nem um nem outro.
Neither one or the other.

Nem isto nem isso.
Neither this nor that.

Nem peixe nem carne.
Neither fish nor fowl.

Nem todos foram.
Not all went.

Nem bem nem mal.	So so. Neither good nor bad.

Não posso nem desejo ir.	I can't go, nor do I want to go.
Não tenho nem tempo nem dinheiro.	I have neither the time nor the money.
Êle não sabe ler nem escrever.	He can't read or write.
Não tenho cigarros nem charutos.	I haven't any cigarettes or cigars.

48. USEFUL WORD GROUPS II

1. Isn't it?

Não é?
Isn't it?

Não é verdade?
Isn't that so?

O português é fácil, não é?
Portuguese is easy, isn't it?

A gente aqui é muito agradável, não é?
People here are very nice, aren't they?

O senhor tem lápis?
Do you have a pencil?

Não tenho.
I don't have any.

É verdade!
That's the truth!

O senhor conhece o Sr. Dias, não é verdade?
You know Mr. Dias, don't you?

Não há nada de verdade nisto.
There's no truth in this.

O senhor vem, não?
You'll come, won't you?

Está frio hoje, não?
It's cold today, isn't it?

A senhora gostou do filme?
Gostei.
Did you like the film?
I liked it.

2. Some, Any, A Few

O senhor tem algum dinheiro?
Do you have any money?

Tenho.
I have (some).

Não, não tenho.
No, I don't have any.

Êle tem dinheiro?
Does he have some money?

Êle tem um pouco.
He has some (a little).

Êle não tem.
He doesn't.

Fica-lhe algum dinheiro?
Do you have any money left?

Fica um pouco.
There's a little left.

Quantos livros tem?
How many books do you have?

Tenho alguns.
I have a few.

Quer algumas peras?
Do you want some pears?

Dê-me algumas.
Give me a few.

QUIZ 19

1. *Não vejo.*	1. Neither this nor that.
2. *Não é nada.*	2. I have no time.
3. *Não me diga!*	3. I don't know where.
4. *Nunca vou.*	4. Nothing happened.
5. *Não o vi.*	5. I don't see.
6. *Acho que não.*	6. I don't know anything.
7. *Não tão depressa.*	7. It's not enough.
8. *Não sei nada.*	8. I didn't see him.
9. *Não vejo nada.*	9. You don't say!
10. *Não é bastante.*	10. He never comes.
11. *Não me importa.*	11. I see nothing.
12. *Não aconteceu nada.*	12. I'll never go.
13. *Êle nunca vem.*	13. It's nothing.
14. *Não é mau.*	14. He's not here.
15. *Nunca irei.*	15. I don't think so.
16. *Êle não está aqui.*	16. It's not bad.
17. *Ninguém vem.*	17. It makes no difference to me.
18. *Nem isto nem isso.*	18. Not so fast.
19. *Não sei onde.*	19. I never go.
20. *Não tenho tempo.*	20. No one comes.

ANSWERS

1—5; 2—13; 3—9; 4—19; 5—8; 6—15; 7—18; 8—6;

9—11; 10—7; 11—17; 12—4; 13—10; 14—16;
15—12; 16—14; 17—20; 18—1; 19—3; 20—2.

LESSON 24

(Useful Word Groups III)

Dê-nos alguns.
Give us some.

Dê-lhe algumas.
Give him a few *(fem.)*.

Alguns dos meus amigos.
Some of my friends.

3. Like, As, How

Como.
Like, as, how

Como eu.
Like me.

Como isso.
Like that.

Como isto.
Like this.

Como nós.
Like us.

Como os outros.
Like the others.

Êste não é como êsse.
This one isn't like that one.

Assim é.
That's the way it is.

Como o senhor quiser.
As you wish.

Êle não é como seu pai (como o pai).[1]
He's not like his father.

Não sei como explicá-lo.
I don't know how to explain it.

Como está? (Como é isso?)
How is it?

É branco como a neve.
It's as white as snow.

Como vai?
How are you?

Como quer que seja.
However it may be.

Seja como fôr.[2]
Be it as it may.

Como falo mal, ninguém me compreende.
As I speak poorly, nobody understands me.

Como? O que disse?
I beg your pardon? What did you say?

Como ela é bonita!
How pretty she is!

---

[1]From now on, the material in parentheses of the recorded text will ordinarily indicate an alternate form which is the one recorded on the Continental Portuguese edition. It will be marked Ⓟ only when it is particularly characteristic of Continental Portuguese as distinguished from Brazilian usage.

[2] **for** Ⓟ.

QUIZ 20

1. *Como o senhor quiser.*	1. He's not like his father.
2. *Como os outros.*	2. What did you say?
3. *Como isto.*	3. Give him a few.
4. *O senhor tem dinheiro?*	4. How pretty she is!
5. *Alguns dos meus amigos.*	5. Do you want some pears?
6. *Êle não é como seu pai.*	6. As you wish.
7. *Como, faz favor?*	7. Do you have any money?
8. *Dê-lhe algumas.*	8. Like the others.
9. *Como ela é bonita!*	9. Like this.
10. *Quer algumas peras?*	10. Some of my friends.

ANSWERS

1—6; 2—8; 3—9; 4—7; 5—10; 6—1; 7—2; 8—3; 9—4; 10—5.

49. HAVE YOU TWO MET?

O senhor conhece o meu amigo?
Do you know my friend?

Acho que já nos conhecemos.
I believe we've met before.

Acho que não tive o prazer.
I believe I haven't had the pleasure.

Não tive o prazer de conhecê-lo.
I haven't had the pleasure of meeting you.

Acho que já se conhecem, não?
I believe you already know each other, don't you?

Claro que nos conhecemos.
Of course we know each other.

Não tive o prazer.
I haven't had the pleasure.

Desejo apresentar-lhe o meu amigo Carlos Gonçalves.
I would like to introduce my friend Charles
    Gonçalves.

50. SMALL TALK

Bom dia.
Good morning.

Como vai? (Como está?)
How are you?

Muito bem. E o senhor?
Very good. And you?

Como vão as coisas?
How is everything?

O que há de nôvo?
What's new?

Nada. Não há nada de nôvo.
Nothing. There's nothing new.

Quase nada.
Almost nothing.

LESSON 25

(Small Talk)

Que lhe tem acontecido que ninguém a vê?
Where have you been lately? ("What has happened
  that no one sees you?")

Tenho estado muito ocupada ùltimamente.
I have been very busy lately.

Não deixe de telefonar-me de vez em quando.
Call me once in a while. ("Don't fail to call me once
  in a while.")

Por que não vem até (a) nossa casa?
Why don't you come by our house?

Vou visitá-los na próxima semana.
I'll call on you next week. ("I am going to visit you
  next week.")

Não (se) esqueça.
Don't forget.

Então, até a próxima semana.
Until next week then.

Passe bem.
Good-by.

51. TAKING LEAVE

Muito prazer em conhecê-la.
Glad to have met you.

O prazer foi todo meu.
The pleasure was (all) mine.

Em breve espero vê-la de nôvo.
I hope to see you again soon.

Aqui tem (o) meu enderêço[1] e (o) meu telefone.
Here's my address and telephone number.

Tem (o) meu enderêço?
Do you have my address?

Não tenho. Tenha a bondade. Muito obrigada.
I don't have it. Please. Thank you.

De nada.
Don't mention it.

Quando posso lhe telefonar (telefonar-lhe)?
When can I call you?

Pela manhã.
In the morning.

Telefono depois de amanhã.
I'll call you day after tomorrow.

Conto com (o) seu telefonema.
I'll be expecting your call.

Até breve.
See you soon.

Até já.
See you soon.

Até logo.
See you soon.

Até a volta.
Until your return.

Até amanhã.
Until tomorrow.

---

[1] **endereço** Ⓟ.

Até sábado.
Until Saturday.

Passe bem.
Good-by.

Adeus.
Good-by.

QUIZ 21

1. Até já.	1. Do you have my address?
2. Adeus.	2. See you tomorrow.
3. Muito prazer em conhecê-lo.	3. I'll be expecting your call.
4. Tem (o) meu enderêço?	4. Until Saturday.
5. Muito prazer.	5. In the morning.
6. Pela manhã.	6. Glad to have met you.
7. Até amanhã.	7. Thank you.
8. Conto com (o) seu telefonema.	8. See you soon.
9. Muito obrigado.	9. Very glad (to have met you).
10. Até sábado.	10. Good-by.

ANSWERS

1—8; 2—10; 3—6; 4—1; 5—9; 6—5; 7—2; 8—3; 9—7; 10—4.

LESSON 26

52. CALLING ON SOMEONE

(Calling on Someone)

O senhor João Dias mora aqui?
Does Mr. John Dias live here?

Mora.
Yes, he does. ("He lives.")

Em que andar?
On what floor?

Terceiro, à esquerda.
Third floor left.

O senhor Dias está em casa?
Is Mr. Dias home?

Não, senhor. Saiu.
No, sir. He's gone out.

A que horas voltará?
What time will he be back?

Não sei lhe dizer (dizer-lhe).
I can't tell you.

Quer deixar um recado?
Do you want to leave a message?

Quero. Pode dar-me lápis e papel?
I do. Can you give me a pencil and some paper?

Volto mais tarde.
I'll be back later.

Volto hoje à noite.
I'll be back tonight.

Volto amanhã.
I'll be back tomorrow.

Volto outro dia.
I'll be back another day.

**Tenha a bondade de lhe dizer (dizer-lhe) que me
    telefone.**
Please tell him to call me.

Vou estar em casa o dia todo.
I'll be home all day.

53. LETTERS AND TELEGRAMS

Gostaria de escrever uma carta.
I'd like to write a letter.

Pode me dar (dar-me) papel?
Can you give me some paper ?

Aqui tem papel e tinta.
Here's some paper and ink.

Vou ao correio.
I'm going to the post office.

Onde vendem selos?
Where do they sell stamps?

Tem selos?
Do you have any stamps?

**Preciso de um sêlo para carta aérea (selo de correio
    aéreo).**
I need an airmail stamp.

Aqui tem selos.
Here are some stamps.

Quero mandar uma carta expressa.
I want to send a special delivery letter.

Quero passar um telegrama.
I want to send a telegram.

Quanto custa um telegrama para Pôrto Alegre?
How much does a telegram to Pôrto Alegre cost?

QUIZ 22

1. *Terceiro, à esquerda.*
2. *Volto mais tarde.*
3. *Mora aqui o senhor João Dias?*
4. *Aqui tem papel e tinta.*
5. *Gostaria de escrever uma carta.*
6. *Tem selos?*
7. *Em que andar?*
8. *Uma carta expressa.*
9. *Vou estar em casa o dia todo.*
10. *Quer deixar um recado?*

1. I'll be home all day.
2. Do you have any stamps?
3. I'd like to write a letter.
4. Do you want to leave a message?
5. What floor?
6. A special delivery letter.
7. Here's some paper and ink.
8. Does Mr. John Dias live here?
9. Third floor left.
10. I'll come back later.

ANSWERS

1—9; 2—10; 3—8; 4—7; 5—3; 6—2; 7—5; 8—6;
9—1; 10—4.

LESSON 27

54. GETTING AROUND

(Getting Around)

Pode me dizer onde é esta rua?
Can you tell me where this street is?

Como se vai a êste enderêço?
How do you get to this address?

É longe?
Is it far?

Qual é o caminho mais curto para a cidade?
Which is the shortest way to the city?

Que caminho devo tomar?
Which road should I take?

Pode me dizer (dizer-me) o caminho para a Rua da Alfândega?
Can you direct me to Alfândega Street?

A Prefeitura (A Câmara Municipal ℗) fica perto daqui?
Is the city hall near here?

Onde há um telefone público?
Where is there a public phone?

Quero dar (fazer) um telefonema.
I want to make a telephone call.

Qual a distância daqui à estação?
How far is the station?

Ainda estamos longe da estação?
Are we still far from the station?

Táxi! Táxi!
Taxi! Taxi!

Está livre?
Are you free?

Leve-me a êste enderêço.
Take me to this address.

Quanto marca o taxímetro?
How much does the meter read?

O ônibus (autocarro ℗) pára aqui?
Does the bus stop here?

O bonde (o carro eléctrico ℗) pára aqui?
Does the streetcar stop here?

Onde devo descer?
Where should I get off?

QUIZ 23

1. *Qual é o caminho mais curto para . . . ?*
2. *Onde há um telefone público?*
3. *Onde é esta rua?*
4. *Leve-me a êste enderêço.*
5. *Qual a distância daqui à estação?*
6. *Fica perto daqui?*
7. *É longe?*
8. *Onde devo descer?*
9. *Como se vai a . . . ?*
10. *O ônibus (autocarro ℗) pára aqui?*

1. How far is the station?
2. How do you get to . . . ?
3. Is it far?

4. Does the bus stop here?
5. Where do I get off?
6. Where is there a public phone?
7. Where is this street?
8. What's the shortest way to get to . . . ?
9. Take me to this address.
10. Is it near here?

ANSWERS

1—8; 2—6; 3—7; 4—9; 5—1; 6—10; 7—3; 8—5;
9—2; 10—4.

55. PLEASE

One of the most common ways of saying "please"
is the equivalent of "Do the favor of": *Faça o favor
(de)*.

Faça o favor de entrar.
Please come in.

Faça o favor de levar isto.
Please carry this.

Faça o favor de vir cedo.
Please come early.

Other polite expressions are:

1. **Faz favor.**
   Please ("do the favor").

   Faz favor de me telefonar (telefonar-me).
   Please telephone me.

Faz favor de sentar-se.
Please sit down.

2. **Tenha a bondade.**
Please ("have the kindness").

Tenha a bondade de preparar tudo.
Please prepare everything.

3. **Por favor.**
Please.

(O) Seu bilhete, por favor.
Your ticket, please.

4. **Queira ...**
Please ...

Queira continuar até domingo.
Please continue until Sunday.

Queira embarcar antes das nove.
Please embark before nine.

Related expressions:

Quero lhe pedir (pedir-lhe) um favor.
I want to ask a favor of you.

Recebi (o) seu favor.
I received your letter ("favor"). (In commercial correspondence.)

Desculpe-me.
Excuse me. (For having done something.)

Desculpe a demora.
Excuse my delay.

QUIZ 24

1. *Faz favor de telefonar-me.*
2. *Faça o favor de vir cedo.*
3. *Faz favor de sentar-se.*
4. *Desculpe a demora.*
5. *Desculpe-me.*
6. *Faça o favor de entrar.*
7. *Tenha a bondade de preparar tudo.*
8. *Faça o favor de levar isto.*
9. *Seu bilhete, por favor.*
10. *Queira continuar até domingo.*

1. Excuse my delay.
2. Excuse me.
3. Please come early.
4. Please carry this.
5. Please continue until Sunday.
6. Your ticket, please.
7. Please sit down.
8. Please come in.
9. Please prepare everything.
10. Please telephone me.

ANSWERS

1—10; 2—3; 3—7; 4—1; 5—2; 6—8; 7—9; 8—4; 9—6; 10—5.

56. SOME USEFUL EXPRESSIONS

1. **Acabar de** means "to have just":

Êle acaba de aceitar.
He just accepted.

Acabo de conseguir a chave.
I have just obtained the key.

Êle acabava de almoçar quando aparecemos.
He had just had lunch when we appeared.

2. **Ter que,** or **ter de** means "to have to":

Tenho que (Tenho de) apressar-me.
I have to hurry.

Você tem de convencer-me primeiro.
You have to convince me first.

3. **Há** means "there is" or "there are":

Há muitos cachorros (cães) nesta cidade.
There are many dogs in this city.

4. **Gostaria de** means "would like to":

Gostaria de ajudar mas não posso.
I'd like to help but I can't.

REVIEW QUIZ 5

1. *Está em* _____ (home, house) *o senhor Dias?*
   a. *andar*
   b. *hora*
   c. *casa*

2. *Quer deixar um* _____ (message)?
   a. *lápis*
   b. *recado*
   c. *papel*

3. *Leve-me a êste* _____ (address).
   a. *cidade*
   b. *caminho*
   c. *endereço*

4. _____ (I need) *um sêlo*.
   a. *vendem*
   b. *preciso de*
   c. *acho*

5. *Não trabalham* _____ (never, ever).
   a. *amanhã*
   b. *nunca*
   c. *sábado*

6. _____ (not) *todos foram*.
   a. *nem*
   b. *nunca*
   c. *hoje*

7. *Dê-me* _____ (some).
   a. *todos*
   b. *algumas*
   c. *nada*

8. *Não tive o prazer de* _____ (meeting you).
   a. *ocupado*
   b. *chamar*
   c. *conhecê-lo*

9. *Tenha a* _____ (goodness) *de preparar tudo*.
   a. *desculpe*
   b. *bondade*
   c. *faça*

10. *Faça o* ____ *de entrar.*
    a. *bondade*
    b. *favor*
    c. *queira*

11. ____ *(please)* *embarcar antes das nove.*
    a. *queira*
    b. *desculpe*
    c. *trabalham*

12. ____ *(I've just)* *de terminar o trabalho.*
    a. *chegar*
    b. *acabo*
    c. *falo*

13. ____ *(I'd like)* *escrever uma carta.*
    a. *gostaria de*
    b. *acaba*
    c. *vai*

14. ____ *(Excuse)* *a demora.*
    a. *tenha*
    b. *desculpe*
    c. *chame*

15. *Não vem* ____ *(nobody).*
    a. *ninguém*
    b. *nada*
    c. *outros*

ANSWERS

1 c.; 2 b.; 3 c.; 4 b.; 5 b.; 6 a.; 7 b.; 8 c.; 9 b.; 10 b.;
11 a.; 12 b.; 13 a.; 14 b.; 15 a.

LESSON 28

(*Who, What, When?*)

57. WHO? WHAT? WHEN?

1. *Quem?* "Who?" "Whom?"

Quem é?	Who is it?
Não sei quem é.	I don't know who it (he) is.
Quem o disse?	Who said it?
Quem disse isso?	Who said that?
De quem é esta bagagem?	Whose baggage is this?
De quem são essas canções?	Whose songs are those?
Para quem é êsse brinquedo?	Who is that toy for?
A quem você entregou (A quem entregou) a máquina fotográfica?	To whom did you deliver the camera?
Com quem brigou?	With whom did you quarrel?
Com quem falaram?	With whom did they speak?
Quem convidaram?	Whom did they invite?

2. *Que?* "What?"

Que é isso?	What is that?
Que é isto?	What is this?
Que aconteceu?	What happened?

Que há de nôvo?[1]	What's new?
Que são?	What are they?
Que horas são?	What time is it?
Que deseja?	What do you want?
Que quer dizer?	What does it mean?
Que dia é hoje?	What day is it today?
Que disse êle?	What did he say?
Que é que êle disse?	What did he say?
Que mais?	What else (more)?
Que é feito da Maria?	What happened to Mary?
Que é que há?	What's wrong?
De que falam?	What are you talking about?
Com que pagam?	What will you pay with?
A que cinema êle foi (foi êle)?	To what movie theatre did he go?

3. *Por que?* "Why?"

Por que você não o alugou?	Why didn't you rent it?
Por que não me disse antes?	Why didn't you tell me before?
Por que não?	Why not?
Por que é tanta pressa?	Why such a hurry?
Por que isso?	Why so?
Por que razão?	For what reason?

4. *Como?* "How?"

Como se diz em português?	How do you say it in Portuguese?

---

[1] nôvo Ⓟ.

Como se chama?	What is your name?
Como se escreve essa palavra?	How is that word spelled (written)?
Como vai?	How are you?
Como se cansou tão cedo?	How did you get tired so early?

5. *Quanto?* "How Much?"

Quanto é?	How much is it?
Quantos cartões recebeu?	How many cards did you receive?
Quantas vêzes o aconselharam?	How many times did they advise it?

LESSON 29

(Liking and Disliking)

6. *Qual?* "What?" "Which?"

Qual deseja o senhor? (Qual deseja?)	Which do you want?
Qual das cadeiras prefere?	Which of the chairs do you prefer?
De qual dos colêtes[1] gosta mais?	Which of the vests do you prefer?
Quais são os costumes que não lhe agradam?	Which are the customs you don't like ("that don't please you")?
Com qual dos irmãos se casou?	Which of the brothers did she marry?

---

[1] coletes Ⓟ.

7. *Onde?* "Where?"

Onde mora o seu cunhado?	Where does your brother-in-law live?
Donde vem êsse barulho?	Where is that noise coming from?
Para onde vão?	Where are they going?

8. *Quando?* "When?"

Quando (se) fecha a biblioteca?	When does the library close?
Quando aconteceu?	When did it happen?
Quando vai êle? (Quando é que êle vai?)	When is he going?
Não sei quando.	I don't know when.
Até quando?	Until when?
Não sei até quando.	I don't know how long (until when).
Desde quando?	Since when?
Para quando?	For when?
Para quando quiser.	For whenever you wish.

QUIZ 25

1. *Como se chama?*	1. When did it happen?
2. *Quantos cartões recebeu?*	2. Since when?
3. *Como se diz em português?*	3. Who is it?
4. *Que disse êle?*	4. Where does he live?
5. *Quando aconteceu?*	5. What's your name?

6. *Desde quando?*	6. What did he say?
7. *Quem é?*	7. Why not?
8. *Por que não?*	8. How do you spell (write) it?
9. *Onde mora?*	9. How many cards did you receive?
10. *Como se escreve?*	10. How do you say it in Portuguese?

ANSWERS

1—5; 2—9; 3—10; 4—6; 5—1; 6—2; 7—3; 8—7; 9—4; 10—8.

REVIEW QUIZ 6

1. *Não vejo* _____ (nothing).
   a. *ninguém*
   b. *nada*
   c. *nunca*

2. *Não vem* _____ (nobody).
   a. *ninguém*
   b. *não*
   c. *nunca*

3. *Não sabe ler* _____ (nor) *escrever.*
   a. *não*
   b. *nunca*
   c. *nem*

4. *O português é fácil* _____ (isn't it?)
   a. *não é*
   b. *não senhor*
   c. *nunca*

5. *Dê-nos* ____ (a few).
   a. *nada*
   b. *alguns*
   c. *algumas vezes*

6. *Quer* ____ (some) *peras?*
   a. *quantos*
   b. *algumas vêzes*
   c. *algumas*

7. *Não é* ____ (like) *seu pai.*
   a. *como*
   b. *isto*
   c. *outros*

8. *Tenho estado muito* ____ (busy) *ùltimamente.*
   a. *sempre*
   b. *ocupado*
   c. *nôvo*

9. *Já se* ____ (know)?
   a. *conhecido*
   b. *conhecem*
   c. *conhecê-lo*

10. *O ônibus (autocarro* Ⓟ*)* ____ (stops) *aqui?*
    a. *pára*
    b. *segunda-feira*
    c. *chama*

11. *Como se vai a êste* ____ (address)?
    a. *correio*
    b. *cartão*
    c. *enderêço*

12. *Não há nada* ____ (new).

    a. *de nôvo*
    b. *nunca*
    c. *prazer*

13. *Acabo de conseguir* ____ (the key).

    a. *o dia*
    b. *a chave*
    c. *a demora*

14. ____ (what) *disse êle?*

    a. *como*
    b. *quando*
    c. *que*

15. ____ (why) *tanta pressa?*

    a. *quando*
    b. *por que*
    c. *onde*

16. ____ (how) *se diz em português?*

    a. *como*
    b. *quando*
    c. *ninguém*

17. ____ (how many) *vêzes o aconselharam?*

    a. *quem*
    b. *quantas*
    c. *como*

18. ____ (who) *disse isso?*

    a. *quem*
    b. *que*
    c. *quando*

19. ____ (where) *mora o seu cunhado?*

    a. *onde*
    b. *como*
    c. *que*

20. ____ (when) *aconteceu?*

    a. *quem*
    b. *qual*
    c. *quando*

ANSWERS

1 b.; 2 a.; 3 c.; 4 a.; 5 b.; 6 c.; 7 a.; 8 b.; 9 b.; 10 a.;
11 c.; 12 a.; 13 b.; 14 c.; 15 b.; 16 a.; 17 b.; 18 a.; 19 a.;
20 c.

58. LIKING AND DISLIKING

1. I Like It

Bom.	Good.
Muito bom.	Very good.
É muito bom.	It's very good.
É ótimo.[1]	It's excellent.
É excelente.	It's excellent.
É estupendo.	It's wonderful.
É magnífico.	It's wonderful.
É perfeito.	It's perfect.
Está bem.	It's all right.
Não é mau.	It's not bad.
Está bem isto?	Is this all right?

---

[1] óptimo Ⓟ.

Muito bem!	Very well! Very good!
Ela é bela.	She's beautiful.
Ela é belíssima.	She's very beautiful.
Ela é muito linda.	She's very pretty.
Ela é encantadora.	She's charming.
Que bonita (que) ela é!	How pretty she is!
Como ela é bonita!	How pretty she is!
Que bom!	How nice!

2. I Don't Like It

Não é bom.	It's not good. It's no good.
Não é muito bom.	It's not very good.
Isso não é bom.	That's no good.
Isto não está bem.	This isn't right. It's not right. This is wrong.
Isso é mau.	That's bad.
É bastante mau.	It's quite bad.
É péssimo.	It's very bad. It's terrible.
É muito ruim.	It's terrible.
Não gosto.	I don't like it.
Não me interessa.	I don't care for it. It doesn't interest me.
Não vale nada.	It's no good. It's worthless.
Não serve para nada.	It's no good. It's worthless.
Não adianta.	It's no use. It's no good.
Que pena!	What a pity!
É horrível!	It's terrible!

QUIZ 26

1.	Está bem.	1.	It's excellent.
2.	Muito bem.	2.	She's very pretty.
3.	É excelente.	3.	It's worthless.
4.	Não é mau.	4.	What a pity!
5.	Isso é mau.	5.	It's no use.
6.	Que pena!	6.	It's wonderful.
7.	Ela é muito linda.	7.	It's all right.
8.	Não vale nada.	8.	That's bad.
9.	Não adianta.	9.	Very well.
10.	É estupendo.	10.	It's not bad.

ANSWERS

1—7; 2—9; 3—1; 4—10; 5—8; 6—4; 7—2; 8—3; 9—5; 10—6.

LESSON 30

(I Like)

3. I Like

Gosto.	I like it.
Gosto muito.	I like it very much.
Gosto...Gosto de...	I like...I like to...
Gosto dêle.	I like him.
Gostamos dela.	We like her.
O senhor gosta?	Do you like it?
Não gosto.	I don't like it.

O senhor gosta da côr?[1]	Do you like the color?
O senhor gosta de Portugal?	Do you like Portugal?
Êles gostam do Brasil.	They like Brazil.
Gostamos dos Estados Unidos.	We like the United States.
O senhor gosta da escôva?[2]	Do you like the brush?
Gosto mais do espelho.	I like the mirror more.
O senhor acha que ela gostará da bôlsa?[3]	Do you think she will like the purse?
Não gostei do primeiro capítulo.	I didn't like the first chapter.
Eu gostaria de me deitar (deitar-me) cedo.	I would like to go to bed early.
Os advogados não gostaram do clube.	The lawyers did not like the club.
Não gostaram nada.	They didn't like it at all.
Gostaria que êles me enviassem um convite.	I would like them to send me an invitation.
Quando quiser.	Whenever you like.
Estou com vontade de lhe escrever (escrever-lhe).	I feel like writing him.
Por que não gosta dêles?	Why don't you like them?
Gosta do quarto?	Do you like the room (bedroom)?

---

[1] cor Ⓟ.
[2] escova Ⓟ.
[3] bolsa Ⓟ.

Gosto.	I like it.
Gosto muito.	I like it very much.
Não gosto.	I don't like it.
Não gosto muito.	I don't like it very much.
Êle gosta mas ela não gosta.	He likes it but she doesn't.
Nós gostamos mas êles não gostam.	We like it but they don't.
Ninguém gosta.	Nobody likes it.
Eu gosto mas (o) João não gosta.	I like it but John doesn't.
Ela gosta de tudo.	She likes everything.

QUIZ 27

1. *Êles não gostaram nada.*	1. I don't like it very much.
2. *O senhor gosta?*	2. Do you like the room?
3. *Gosto muito.*	3. They like Brazil.
4. *O senhor gosta da côr?*	4. We like her.
5. *Quando quiser.*	5. Nobody likes it.
6. *Êles gostam do Brasil.*	6. I like it very much.
7. *Ninguém gosta.*	7. Do you like it?
8. *Gostamos dela.*	8. Whenever you like.
9. *Não gosto muito.*	9. They didn't like it at all.
10. *O senhor gosta do quarto?*	10. Do you like the color?

ANSWERS

1—9; 2—7; 3—6; 4—10; 5—8; 6—3; 7—5; 8—4; 9—1; 10—2.

59. IN, TO, FROM

Estive em Brasília.	I was in Brasilia.
Vou a Lisboa.	I am going to Lisbon.
Venho de Coimbra.	I come (am) from Coimbra.
Parto para São Paulo.	I'm leaving for São Paulo.
Cheguei até Belo Horizonte.	I got as far as Belo Horizonte.

---

1. *A* "to"

À direita.	To the right.
À esquerda.	To the left.
Pouco a pouco.	Little by little.
A pé.	On foot.
À mão.	By hand.
Ao meio-dia.	At noon.
À meia-noite.	At midnight.
A meu ver.	In my opinion.
Puseram-se à mesa.	They sat down at the table.
A que horas?	At what time?
À americana.	In the American way.
A respeito de.	Regarding, with respect to.
Êle ficou à porta.	He stayed at the door.
Êle o fêz (fê-lo Ⓟ)[1] à fôrça.	He did it by force.

---

[1] See item 5 of section 20 of grammar summary.

LESSON 31

(Useful Word Groups IV)

2. *Com* "with"

Café com leite.	Coffee with milk.
Ela foi com o estudante.	She went with the student.
Estou com fome.	I am hungry.

3. *De* "of," "from"

É de meu tio.	It's from my uncle.
Venho do Rio de Janeiro.	I come (am) from Rio de Janeiro.
É de pedra.	It's made of stone.
De dia e de noite.	By day and by night.
De nôvo.	Again.

4. *Em* "in"

Vivi em Portugal dois anos.	I lived in Portugal two years.
Saio dentro de quatro dias.	I'm leaving in four days.
Em lugar de.	Instead of.
Em fim.	Finally.

5. *Até* "up to," "until"

Até o (ao) Estoril.	Up to (as far as) Estoril.
Subi até o quinto andar.	I went up to the fifth floor.
Até amanhã.	Until tomorrow.
Até logo.	See you later. (See you soon.)

Até já.	See you soon.
Até a vista.	See you later.

6. *Desde* "from"

Desde aqui.	From here.
Desde que o vi.	Since I saw him.
Desde quando?	Since when?

7. *Sôbre*[1] "on," "over"

Sôbre a mesa.	On the table.
Que disseram sôbre o assunto?	What did they say about the subject?

8. *Por* "for," "through"

Sessenta milhas por hora.	Sixty miles an hour.
Eu o comprei (comprei-o) por um dólar.	I bought it for a dollar.
Eu lhe dei (dei-lhe) vinte cruzeiros pela bôlsa.	I gave him twenty cruzeiros for the purse.
Êle me deu o seu livro pelo meu.	He gave me his book for mine.
Passamos pela Espanha.	We passed through Spain.
Êle entrou pela porta.	He came in through the door.
Eu vou por êle.	I'll go for (in place of) him.

---

[1] sobre Ⓟ.

Other Expressions:

Por quê?	Why?
Por agora.	For the time being.
Pela manhã.	In the morning.
Por acaso.	By chance.
Por exemplo.	For example.
Por isso.	For that reason. Therefore.
Por meio de.	By means of.
Por causa de.	On account of.
Por fim.	Finally. At last.
Por aqui.	This way. Around here.
Está por fazer.	It's still to be done.
Por atacado.	Wholesale.
Por certo.	Certainly.
Por assim dizer.	So to speak.
Por conseguinte.	Consequently. Therefore.
Por bem ou por mal.	For better or for worse.
Por escrito.	In writing.
Por·Deus!	For heaven's sake!
Por enquanto.	For the time being.
Por pouco.	Almost.
Por interessante que seja.	However interesting it may be.
Por volta das duas.	Around two o'clock.

9. *Para* "for," "in order to"
   Para indicates direction, purpose:

Para ir lá.	To go there.
Uma estante para livros.	A bookcase ("a stand for books").

Êle partiu para Belém.	He left for Belém.
A carta é para ela.	The letter is for her.
A lição para amanhã.	The lesson for tomorrow.
Para êle é fácil.	It's easy for him.
Não serve pàra nada.	It's worthless. It's not good for anything.
Para lá e para cá.	Back and forth.
Para onde êles foram?	Where did they go?
Para que você o faz?	Why do you do it? (For what reason do you do it?)
Para sempre.	Forever. For always.
Descrevo com detalhes para que compreendam bem.	I am describing it in detail so that they may understand it well.
Estamos prontos para a viagem.	We are ready for the trip.

With *estar* it means "about to":

Estamos para sair.	We are about to leave. We are leaving.

QUIZ 28

1. *Ao meio-dia.*	1. On foot.
2. *Pouco a pouco.*	2. In my opinion.
3. *À direita.*	3. I come from Rio de Janeiro.
4. *À americana.*	4. It's made of stone.
5. *Com.*	5. By day and by night.
6. *A pé.*	6. Again.
7. *Venho do Rio de Janeiro.*	7. On the table.

8. *É de pedra.*	8. To the right.
9. *A respeito de.*	9. For example.
10. *De nôvo.*	10. Little by little.
11. *Por exemplo.*	11. Until tomorrow.
12. *De dia e de noite.*	12. At noon.
13. *À esquerda.*	13. Since I saw him.
14. *A meu ver.*	14. In the American way.
15. *Até o (ao) Estoril.*	15. With.
16. *Saio dentro de quatro dias.*	16. Instead of.
17. *Sôbre a mesa.*	17. To the left.
18. *Até amanhã.*	18. Regarding.
19. *Em lugar de.*	19. As far as Estoril.
20. *Desde que o vi.*	20. I'm leaving in four days.

ANSWERS

1—12; 2—10; 3—8; 4—14; 5—15; 6—1; 7—3; 8—4; 9—18; 10—6; 11—9; 12—5; 13—17; 14—2; 15—19; 16—20; 17—7; 18—11; 19—16; 20—13.

QUIZ 29

1. *Por acaso.*	1. I bought it for a dollar.
2. *Por volta das duas.*	2. Sixty miles an hour.
3. *Passamos pela Espanha.*	3. Certainly.
4. *Por agora.*	4. For that reason.
5. *Eu o comprei por um dólar.*	5. Around here.
6. *Por isso.*	6. For heaven's sake!

7. Sessenta milhas por hora.
8. Por certo.
9. Até logo.
10. Por Deus!
11. Por fim.
12. Êle entrou pela porta.
13. Por aqui.
14. Por assim dizer.
15. Está por fazer.

7. At last.
8. By chance.
9. It's still to be done.
10. For the time being.
11. See you soon.
12. Around two o'clock.
13. So to speak.
14. He came in through the door.
15. We passed through Spain.

ANSWERS

1—8; 2—12; 3—15; 4—10; 5—1; 6—4; 7—2; 8—3; 9—11; 10—6; 11—7; 12—14; 13—5; 14—13; 15—9.

QUIZ 30

1. A carta é para ela.
2. Não serve para nada.
3. A lição para amanhã.
4. Estamos para sair.
5. Para sempre.
6. Uma estante para livros.
7. Para ir lá.
8. Êle partiu para Belém.
9. Estamos prontos para a viagem.
10. Para onde êles foram?

1. A bookcase.
2. The lesson for tomorrow.
3. To go there.
4. He left for Belém.
5. Where did they go?
6. We are ready for the trip.
7. The letter is for her.
8. Forever.
9. It's worthless.
10. We are about to leave.

ANSWERS

1—7; 2—9; 3—2; 4—10; 5—8; 6—1; 7—3; 8—4;
9—6; 10—5.

LESSON 32

60. ASKING YOUR WAY

(Asking Your Way)

Por favor.
Excuse me. Please.

Como se chama esta cidade?
What is the name of this town?

A que distância estamos de Pôrto Alegre?
How far are we from Pôrto Alegre?

Quantos quilômetros são daqui a Sintra?
How many kilometers is it from here to Sintra?

Fica a dez quilômetros daqui.
It's ten kilometers from here.

Como se vai daqui a Braga?
How do I (does one) get to Braga from here?

Siga êste caminho.
Follow this road.

Pode dizer-me como ir a êste enderêço?
Can you tell me how I can get to this address?

Sabe onde fica êste lugar?
Do you know where this place is?

Como se chama esta rua?
What is the name of this street?

Pode dizer-me onde fica esta rua?
Can you tell me where this street is?

Onde é a Rua da Liberdade?
Where is Liberdade Street (Liberty Street)?

Fica longe daqui?
Is it far from here?

Fica perto?
Is it near?

É a terceira rua à direita.
It's the third street to the right.

Passe por aqui.
Go this way.

Siga sempre em frente.
Go straight ahead.

Siga até a esquina e dobre (vire Ⓟ) à esquerda.
Go to the corner and turn to the left.

Dobre (Vire Ⓟ) à direita.
Turn right.

Onde há uma garage Ⓑ (garagem Ⓑ and Ⓟ)?
Where is there a garage?

Está aberta a garage (garagem)?
Is the garage open?

Onde é o pôsto[1] policial (a esquadra Ⓟ)?
Where is the police station?

Onde é a Prefeitura (a Câmara Municipal Ⓟ)?
Where is the City Hall?

Onde pára o ônibus (o autocarro Ⓟ)?
Where does the bus stop?

---

[1] **posto** Ⓟ.

Onde devo descer?
Where do I get off?

Em que parada (paragem Ⓟ) devo descer?
At what stop should I get off?

Onde fica a estação da estrada (do caminho Ⓟ) de ferro?
Where is the railroad station?

Qual é o trem (o comboio Ⓟ) para a capital?
Which is the train to the capital?

De que plataforma sai?
From which platform does it leave?

Onde está o guichê (guichet Ⓟ) de informações?
Where is the information desk?

Tenha a bondade de dar-me um horário.
Please give me a timetable.

A que horas sai?
At what time does it leave?

Acaba de sair.
It just left.

Vai sair agora.
It's going to leave now.

A que horas sai o próximo trem (comboio Ⓟ)?
At what time does the next train leave?

A que horas sai o expresso (o rápido)?
At what time does the express leave?

A que horas chega à capital?
At what time does it arrive in the capital?

Tem carro dormitório? (Tem carruagem cama? Ⓟ)
Does it have a sleeper?

Não, mas tem carro (vagão) restaurante e carro para fumar (fumadores Ⓟ).
No, but it has a diner and a smoking car.

Tem ar condicionado?
Is it air-conditioned?

Onde fica o guichê de passagens (a bilheteira Ⓟ)?
Where is the ticket window?

Por favor, uma passagem para São Paulo.
A ticket to São Paulo, please.

Simples ou de ida e volta?
One way or round trip?

De ida e volta; é mais barato, não é?
Round trip; it's cheaper, isn't it?

É. De primeira ou (de) segunda classe?
Yes, it is. First or second class?

De primeira. Quanto é?
First-class. How much is it?

Tenho pouca bagagem. Só duas malas.
I have only a little baggage. Just two bags.

LESSON 33

(Writing, Phoning, Telegraphing)

Um pouco mais de uma hora.
A little more than an hour.

Êste lugar está ocupado?
Is this seat taken?

Vou pôr a mala aqui.
I'm going to put my bag here.

Que estação é esta?
What station is this?

Quanto tempo demoramos aqui?
How long do we stay (stop) here?

Temos de baldear aqui?
Do we have to change trains here?

Êste trem (comboio Ⓟ) pára na capital?
Does this train stop in the capital?

61. WRITING, PHONING, TELEGRAPHING

O senhor tem (um) lápis?
Do you have a pencil?

O senhor tem (uma) caneta?
Do you have a pen?

Tenho uma caneta-tinteiro e uma caneta esferográfica.
I have a fountain pen and a ballpoint pen.

O senhor tem mata-borrão?
Do you have a blotter?

Não tenho envelopes.
I don't have any envelopes.

Nem selos.
Nor stamps.

Desejo mandar uma carta aérea (uma carta por avião).
I want to send an airmail letter.

Onde é o correio?
Where is the post office?

Na esquina.
On the corner.

Onde vendem selos?
Where do they sell stamps?

Quero enviar esta carta pelo correio aéreo (esta carta por avião).
I want to send this letter airmail.

Quanto é o porte?
How much is the postage?

Gostaria de passar um telegrama.
I'd like to send a telegram.

Onde é o telégrafo?
Where is the telegraph office?

Fica no correio.
It's in the post office.

Quanto é um telegrama para São Paulo?
How much is a telegram to São Paulo?

Quanto tempo leva para chegar?
How long does it take to get there?

Há telefone aqui?
Is there a telephone here?

Onde posso telefonar?
Where can I phone?

Onde fica (está) o telefone?
Where is the telephone?

Onde há uma cabina telefônica?[1]
Where is there a telephone booth?

No vestíbulo do hotel.
In the hotel lobby.

**Dá licença para usar o telefone? (Dá licença que eu use
o telefone?)**
May I use your phone? ("Will you give permission to
use the telephone?")

Pois não!
Of course!

Quero dar (fazer) um telefonema interurbano.
I want to make a long-distance call.

Quanto custa um telefonema para Lisboa?
How much is a phone call to Lisbon?

Quero falar com o sete-cinco-oito-dois.
I want 7582.

Espere um momento.
Hold the wire a minute. ("Wait a moment.")

A linha está ocupada (impedida Ⓟ).
The line is busy.

Telefonista, deu-me o número errado.
Operator, you gave me the wrong number.

Não respondem.
There is no answer.

Gostaria de falar (Desejo falar) com o senhor Silva.
I'd like to speak to Mr. Silva.

---

[1] **telefónica** Ⓟ.

Fala o senhor Silva.
This is Mr. Silva.

Aqui fala o senhor Martins.
This is Mr. Martins speaking.

Com quem falo?
Who is this? ("With whom am I speaking?")

Com o senhor Martins.
With Mr. Martins.

LESSON 34

62. FAMILY AFFAIRS

(Family Affairs)

Como se chama o senhor? (Como se chama?)
What is your name?

Chamo-me João Martins.
My name is João (John) Martins.

Como se chama êle?
What is his name?

Êle se chama (Chama-se) Carlos Magalhães.
His name is Carlos (Charles) Magalhães.

Como se chama ela?
What is her name?

Ela se chama (Ela chama-se) Maria Fernandes.
Her name is Maria (Mary) Fernandes.

Como se chamam êles?
What are their names?

Êle se chama (chama-se) José Campos e ela Ana Coelho.
His name is José (Joseph) Campos and hers is Ana Coelho.

Qual é o nome dêle?
What is his name?

O nome dêle é Carlos.
His name is Carlos.

Qual é o seu nome de família?
What is his last name?

É Silva. (Silva.)
It's Silva.

Donde é o senhor?
Where are you from?

Sou de Lisboa.
I'm from Lisbon.

Onde nasceu o senhor? (Onde nasceu?)
Where were you born?

Nasci em Coimbra.
I was born in Coimbra.

Quantos anos o senhor tem? (Quantos anos tem?)
How old are you?

Tenho vinte e quatro anos.
I am twenty-four years old.

Eu faço (Faço) vinte e cinco anos em setembro.
I'll be twenty-five in September.

Nasci em dezenove (dezanove Ⓟ) de agôsto de mil novecentos e quarenta e seis.
I was born August 19, 1946.

Quantos irmãos o senhor tem? (Quantos irmãos tem?)
How many brothers do you have?

Tenho dois irmãos.
I have two brothers.

O mais velho tem dezessete (dezassete Ⓟ) anos.
The older one is seventeen.

Êle estuda na universidade. (É estudante da universidade.)
He's at (he studies at) the university.

O mais nôvo tem quinze anos.
The younger one is fifteen.

Êle está (Está) no último ano do curso secundário.
He's in the last year of high school.

Quantas irmãs o senhor tem? (Quantas irmãs tem?)
How many sisters do you have?

Tenho uma irmã.
I have one sister.

Ela tem nove anos. (Tem nove anos.)
She's nine.

Ela está numa escola primária. (Anda na escola primária.)
She goes to grammar (primary) school.

O que é (o) seu pai?
What does your father do?

É advogado.
He's a lawyer.

É arquiteto (arquitecto).
He's an architect.

É professor.
He's a teacher.

É professor universitário.
He's a university professor.

É médico.
He's a doctor.

É comerciante.
He's a businessman.

É fazendeiro Ⓑ (lavrador).
He's a farmer.

É funcionário público.
He's in the government service.

É operário.
He's a worker.

Êle trabalha (Trabalha) numa fábrica de automóveis.
He works in an automobile factory.

Quando é o seu aniversário?
When is your birthday?

Meu (O meu) aniversário é daqui a duas semanas (em vinte e três de janeiro).
My birthday is in two weeks (January 23rd).

Tem parentes aqui?
Do you have any relatives here?

Tôda[1] a sua família mora aqui?
Does all your family live here?

Tôda a família menos (os) meus avós.
All my family except my grandparents.

Êles moram numa fazenda perto de Belo Horizonte.
They live on a farm near Belo Horizonte.

O senhor é parente do senhor Oliveira?
Are you related to Mr. Oliveira?

É meu tio.
He's my uncle.

É meu primo.
He's my cousin.

O senhor é parente da senhora Nunes?
Are you related to Mrs. Nunes?

É minha tia.
She's my aunt.

É minha prima.
She's my cousin.

---

[1] **toda** Ⓟ.

LESSON 35

63. COMPRAS

SHOPPING

(Buying Things. Ordering Breakfast)

1. **Quanto custa isto?**
   How much is this?

2. **Dez cruzeiros (escudos Ⓟ).**
   Ten cruzeiros (escudos).

3. **É muito caro. Não tem alguma coisa mais barata?**
   That's rather expensive. Haven't you anything cheaper?

4. **Do mesmo gênero?[1]**
   Of the same kind?

5. **Do mesmo ou de outro parecido.**
   Of the same or something similar.

6. **Tem êste.**
   There's this.

7. **Não tem alguma coisa de outra espécie que me possa mostrar?**
   Haven't you any other kind you could show me?

8. **De menos preço?**
   Less expensive?

9. **Se é possível.**
   If possible.

---

[1] gênero Ⓟ.

10. **Talvez isto seja o que quer.**
   Perhaps this is what you want.

11. **Depende do preço.**
   That depends on the price.

12. **Êste custa oito cruzeiros (escudos Ⓟ).**
   This one is eight cruzeiros (escudos).

13. **Gosto mais do que do outro.**
   I like it better than the other one.

14. **É mais barato.**
   It's cheaper.

15. **E êste outro, é mais barato ou mais caro?**
   How about this one; is it cheaper or more expensive?

16. **É mais caro.**
   It's more expensive.

17. **Não tem mais alguma coisa em estoque (em existência Ⓟ)?**
   Haven't you anything else in stock?

18. **Em breve espero receber novos estilos.**
   (Espero receber em breve novos modelos. Ⓟ)
   I'm hoping to receive some new styles soon.

19. **Para quando?**
   How soon?

20. **De um dia para o outro. Pode passar (por aqui) lá pelo fim da semana?**
   Any day now. Can you drop in toward the end of the week?

21. **Posso. . . . E qual é o preço disto?**
   Yes, I can. . . . What's the price of this?

22. **Cinco cruzeiros (escudos Ⓟ) o par.**
    Five cruzeiros (escudos) a pair.

23. **Quero uma dúzia.**
    I'd like to have a dozen.

24. **Quer levar consigo?**
    Will you take them with you?

25. **Prefiro¹ que os envie.**
    I'd rather have you send them.

26. **O enderêço é o mesmo de sempre?**
    Is the address still the same?

27. **O mesmo.**
    The same.

28. **Até logo.**
    Good-by.

29. **Passe bem.**
    Good-by.

NOTES

Title: *Compras* "Purchases."²

1.³ *Quanto custa isto?* ("How much does this cost?").
How much is this? You can also say: *Quanto é?*
How much is it? *Por quanto se vende isto?* ("At,
or for how much is this sold?") How much is
this? *Por quanto se vendem os limões?* ("For how

---

¹ **Prefiro** is from *preferir*, a radical-changing verb. See grammar summary section 41, part III.

² Words in quotation marks are literal translations.

³ Numbers refer to the sentences above.

much are the lemons sold?") How much are the lemons? *Quanto lhe custaram as calças?* ("How much did the trousers cost to you?") How much did your trousers cost?

2. The cruzeiro is the currency unit of Brazil. formerly having been the *mil réis.* Its value has varied greatly due to steep inflation. As of this writing. the exchange rate is approximately 8,200 cruzeiros to the dollar. The escudo is the currency unit of Portugal. The present rate of exchange is 165 escudos to the dollar.

3. *É muito caro.* ("It's very expensive.") That's rather expensive. *Isto é muito caro.* This is very high (expensive). *Barato* cheap. *Mais barato* ("More cheap") Cheaper. (See secton 18 of the Summary. of Portuguese Grammar.) *Muito barato* very cheap.

4. *Gênero,* kind, class, sort.

6. *Tem êste.* ("You have, or there is, this one.") There's this (one), or, we have this (one).

7. "Don't you have something of another kind you could show me?" *Mostre-me outra coisa.* ("Show me another thing.") Show me something else.

8. "Of less price?"

10. *Seja* from *ser* (see section 39 of the grammar summary).—"Perhaps this one is what you want."

11. *Depender de,* to depend on.

15. *E êste outro.* "And this other one."

18. *Em breve,* in brief; in a short time.

19. *Para quando?* "For when?"

20. *De um dia para o outro.* "From one day to the other." *Passar (por aqui)* to pass (by here, to stop in).

21. *Posso* I can. In answer to a question, often just the verb will be repeated without "yes" or "no." *Pode passar por aqui? Posso. Pode vir amanhã?* Can you come tomorrow? *Não posso.* No, I can't. ("I can't.")

24. *Consigo* is a combination which comes from *com* "with" and *si* "oneself," "yourself," etc. One also hears *com o senhor* or *com a senhora* for "with you."

25. *Prefiro que* . . . I prefer that, I'd prefer that, or I'd rather . . .

26. "The address is the same of (as) always?"

28. and 29. For other expressions on departure see Lesson 8.

QUIZ 31

1. *É muito* _____ (expensive).

    a. *custa*

    b. *isto*

    c. *caro*

2. *Não tem alguma coisa mais* _____ (cheap)?

    a. *gênero*

    b. *preço*

    c. *barata*

3. *Do* _____ (same) *gênero.*

    a. *alguma coisa*

    b. *mesmo*

    c. *mais*

4. *De* _____ (less) *preço.*

    a. *mais*

    b. *menos*

    c. *mesmo*

5. *Gosto* ____ (more) *do que do outro.*
   a. *custa*
   b. *mais*
   c. *mesmo*

6. *Não* ____ (have) *mais alguma coisa?*
   a. *tem*
   b. *caro*
   c. *outro*

7. *Espero* ____ (receive) *novos estilos (novos modelos).*
   a. *custar*
   b. *levar*
   c. *receber*

8. *Para* ____ (when)?
   a. *estoque*
   b. *caro*
   c. *quando* .

9. *O* ____ (address) *é o mesmo de sempre?*
   a. *enderêço*
   b. *escudo*
   c. *envie*

ANSWERS

1 c.; 2 c.; 3 b.; 4 b.; 5 b.; 6 a.; 7 c.; 8 c.; 9 a.

64. O CAFÉ DA MANHÃ Ⓑ
(O PEQUENO ALMOÇO Ⓟ)
BREAKFAST

1. P[1]: **Você está com fome? (Você tem fome?)**
P: Are you hungry?

2. J: **Estou. (Tenho.)**
J: Yes, I am.

3. M: **Eu tenho uma fome canina. (Tenho uma fome canina.)**
M: I'm terribly hungry.

4. P: **Garçom! Garçom!** Ⓑ **(Empregado! Empregado!** Ⓟ**)**
P: Waiter! Waiter!

5. G: **Às suas ordens. Que desejam?**
G: At your service. What would you like?

6. P: **Desejamos o café da manhã (o pequeno almoço) para três pessoas.**
P: We'd like breakfast for three.

7. M: **Que pode nos servir (servir-nos)?**
M: What do you have?

8. G: **Café com leite, chá, chocolate . . .**
G: Coffee with milk, tea, chocolate . . .

9. P: **O que servem com o café?**
P: What do you serve with it?

---

[1] *P.* stands here for *Pedro* "Peter"; *J.* for *João* "John"; *M.* for *Maria* "Mary"; *G.* for *Garçom* "Waiter."

10. G: Pão, torradas . , .
G: Bread, toast . . .

11. M: E manteiga?
M: And butter?

12. G: Sim, também.
G: Yes, also.

13. J: Quero uma xícara (chávena Ⓟ) de café com leite, e pão.
J: I'd like a cup of coffee with milk, and some bread (rolls).

14. P: Quero o mesmo.
P: I'd like the same.

15. J: Maria, você o que quer? (Maria, o que quer?)
J: Mary, what do you want?

16. M: Eu não quero muita coisa.
M: I don't want very much.

17. J: Quer se conservar (conservar-se) esbelta, não (é)?
J: You're watching your figure, aren't you?

18. M: Não precisamente. É mais um hábito.
M: Not exactly. It's more of a habit.

19. G: E a senhorita, o que quer? (A senhora, o que quer?)
G: And what will you have, miss?

20. M: Chá e um ôvo[1] quente.
M: Tea and a soft-boiled egg.

---

[1] ovo Ⓟ.

21. **J: Garçom,[1] queira me trazer um guardanapo. (Queira trazer-me um guardanapo.)**
    J: Waiter, please bring me a napkin.

22. **M: E para mim um garfo, por favor.**
    M: And a fork for me, please.

23. **P: Tenha a bondade de nos trazer (trazer-nos) mais açúcar.**
    P: Please bring us some more sugar.

24. **J: E depois, a conta . . . Aqui tem, garçom,[1] fique com o trôco.[2]**
    J: And then, the check. . . . Here you are, waiter. Keep the change.

25. **G: Muito obrigado, senhor.**
    G: Thank you, sir.

NOTES

1. *Você está com fome?* ("Are you with hunger?") *Você tem fome?* ("Do you have hunger?") Are you hungry?

2. *Eu tenho uma fome canina.* ("I have a canine hunger.") I'm terribly hungry. *Cão* and *cachorro* are words for "dog." *Tenho* (I have) is from *ter* to have (see section 43 of the grammar summary).

4. *Garçon* and *garção* are also used.

5. *Às suas ordens.* ("At your orders.") At your service. *Que desejam?* ("What do you want?") What would you like?

6. *O café da manhã* ("The coffee of the morning") Breakfast. (Used in Brazil, where it is also

---

[1] Recorded only on the Brazilian edition.
[2] troco Ⓟ.

shortened to *o café*.) *O pequeno almoço* ("The small lunch") and *o primeiro almoço* ("The first lunch") Breakfast. (Used in Portugal.)

7. "What can you serve us?" The *nos* may come before the infinitive *servir*, or after it, joined with a hyphen (see item 2 b. of section 20 of the grammar summary).

10. *Pão* is bread, but in a general sense it can also include rolls. *Pãozinho* means roll, plural *pãezinhos*.

17. "You want to stay slender." *Não?* ("No?"), *Não é?* ("Isn't it?"), are short forms of *Não é verdade?* ("Isn't it true?")

19. "And what does the young lady want?"

20. *Ôvo* egg. *Ovos quentes* soft-boiled eggs. *Ovos estrelados* fried eggs. *Ovos mexidos* scrambled eggs. *Ovos duros* hard-boiled eggs.

23. "Have the kindness to bring me more sugar."

24. *Fique com o trôco.* ("Remain with the change.") Keep the change. The verb *ficar* to stay, remain, is used in a variety of expressions with an extension of meaning, often being the equivalent of "to be." *Ficou em casa* he stayed home. *Onde fica?* Where is it? *Fico convencido.* I am convinced. *Êles ficam em pé.* They are standing. *Êsse paletó lhe fica bem.* That jacket looks good on you. *Fiquei doente.* I became ill. *Ela ficou zangada.* She was (became) angry.

25. "Much obliged."

QUIZ 32

1. ____ (We want) *o café da manhã (o pequeno almoço) para três pessoas.*
   a. *desejamos*
   b. *conservamos*
   c. *fome*

2. ____ (and) *manteiga?*
   a. *a*
   b. *e*
   c. *ôvo*

3. *Quero o* ____ (same).
   a. *muito*
   b. *mesmo*
   c. *servem*

4. *O que* ____ (do you want)?
   a. *tenho*
   b. *tem*
   c. *quer*

5. *Eu não quero* ____ (much).
   a. *fome*
   b. *mesmo*
   c. *muita coisa*

6. *Queira* ____ (bring me) *um guardanapo.*
   a. *costume*
   b. *me trazer (trazer-me)*
   c. *mesmo*

7. *E* ____ (then, later) *a conta.*
   a. *amanhã*
   b. *garfo*
   c. *depois*

ANSWERS

1 a.; 2 b.; 3 b.; 4 c.; 5 c.; 6 b.; 7 c.

65. A SAMPLE MENU
CARDÁPIO (EMENTA ℗) MENU

Canja ou sopa de cebola	Chicken-rice soup or onion soup
Omeleta	Omelet
Bacalhau	Cod
Frango assado	Roast chicken
Costeletas grelhadas	Grilled chops
Bife com batatas fritas	Steak with fried potatoes
Salada de alface com tomate	Lettuce and tomato salad
Queijo e frutas	Cheese and fruit
Café	Coffee

LESSON 36

66. PROCURANDO APARTAMENTO
APARTMENT HUNTING

(Apartment Hunting)

1. Venho ver o apartamento.
I've come to see ("I come to see") the apartment.

2. Qual dêles?
Which one?

3. **Aquêle que está para alugar.**
The one which is for rent.

4. **Tem Ⓑ (há) dois.**
There are two.

5. **O senhor pode me dar (dar-me) alguns detalhes (algumas informações)?**
Can you describe them?

6. **O do quinto andar não tem mobília.**
The one on the fifth floor is unfurnished.

7. **E o outro?**
And the other one?

8. **O do segundo andar é mobiliado (mobilado).**
The one on the second floor is furnished.

9. **Quantas peças (divisões Ⓟ) têm?**
How many rooms do they have?

10. **O do quinto andar tem quatro peças (divisões), cozinha e banheiro (casa de banho Ⓟ).**
The one on the fifth floor has four rooms, a kitchen and a bathroom.

11. **Dá para a rua?**
Does it face the street?

12. **Não, dá para o pátio.**
No, it faces the courtyard.

13. **E o do segundo andar?**
And what about the one on the second floor?

14. O do segundo andar tem um quarto, sala de estar, e sala de jantar.
The one on the second floor has a bedroom, a living room, and a dining room.

15. Também dá para o pátio?
Does it also look out on the courtyard?

16. Não, dá para a rua.
No, it faces the street.

17. Quanto é o aluguel (a renda Ⓟ)?
How much is the rent?

18. O aluguel do maior é vinte e cinco mil cruzeiros por mês, mais a água e o gás. (A renda do maior é mil e quinhentos escudos por mês, além da água e do gás.Ⓟ)
The larger one rents for twenty-five thousand cruzeiros a month, plus water and gas. (The larger one rents for fifteen hundred escudos a month, besides water and gas. Ⓟ)

19. E o apartamento mobiliado (mobilado)?
And the furnished apartment?

20. Êste se aluga por quarenta mil cruzeiros por mês, tudo incluído. (Este aluga-se por três mil escudos, tudo incluído. Ⓟ)
That one rents for forty thousand cruzeiros everything included. (That one rents for three thousand escudos, everything included. Ⓟ)

21. Como é a mobília?
How is the furniture?

22. **Os móveis são modernos e estão em boas condições.**
It's modern furniture and it's in excellent condition.

23. **Estão incluídos a roupa de cama e o serviço de mesa?**
Are bed linens and silverware included?

24. **A senhora achará tudo o que precisar, até utensílios de cozinha.**
You'll find everything you need, even kitchen utensils.

25. **É preciso assinar um contrato?**
Does one have to sign a lease?

26. **Para isso a senhora terá que falar com o administrador.**
You'll have to speak to the renting agent about that.

27. **Quais são as condições?**
What are the terms?

28. **Um mês adiantado e outro de depósito.**
One month's rent in advance and another as a deposit.

29. **É tudo?**
Is that all?

30. **Naturalmente, a senhora terá que dar referências.**
Of course, you will have to give references.

31. **A propósito, tem elevador?**
By the way, is there an elevator?

32. Não, não tem.
No, there isn't.

33. É pena.
That's too bad.

34. Além disso, o prédio é muito moderno.
Aside from that, the building is very modern.

35. Que quer dizer com isso?
What do you mean?

36. Tem aquecimento central e escada de serviço.
There's central heating and a back stairway.

37. Tem água quente?
Is there hot water?

38. Naturalmente. Os banheiros foram remodelados recentemente. (As casas de banho foram remodeladas recentemente. (P))
Of course! The bathrooms were remodeled recently.

39. Ah, esquecia . . . Tem quarto para a empregada?
Oh, I forgot—is there a room for the maid?

40. Tem, e muito bom.
Yes, ("and") a very good one.

41. Podemos ver os apartamentos?
May we see the apartments?

42. Só pela manhã.
Only in the morning.

43. Muito bem. Venho amanhã pela manhã. Muito obrigada.
Very well. I'll come tomorrow morning. Thank you very much.

44. De nada. Às suas ordens.
Don't mention it. At your service.

NOTES

Title: *Procurando apartamento*. Looking for an apartment.

2. "Which of them?"

3. *Aquêle* "that one." *Alugar* to rent, to lease, to let, to hire.

5. "Can you give me some details (some information)?"

6. "The one of the fifth floor does not have furniture." *Móveis* also means furniture. *Desmobiliado (Desmobilado)* unfurnished.

9. *Peças* has a variety of meanings. Here it means "rooms" in the sense of units. The word also means piece, portion, section, a play (theatre), etc. *Quarto* and *sala* are used for rooms of the house. *Quarto* will often have the meaning of bedroom or sleeping quarters. *Divisão* ("division") can mean "room" in Portugal.

10. *Banho* bath. *Banheiro* Ⓑ bathroom, *banheira* bathtub, *chuveiro* shower, *tomar banho de chuveiro* to take a shower. *Casa* ("house") can mean "room" in Portugal: *casa de banho* bathroom.

11. *Dá* is from the verb *dar* to give.

13. "And the one of the second floor?"

14. *Quarto* bedroom; also *quarto de dormir*. Sometimes *o living* is heard for living room.

18. "The rent of the larger one is . . ."

20. "This one is rented for . . ."

22. "The furniture is modern . . ." Notice that *mobília*

takes a singular verb; *móveis* takes a plural verb; *móvel* is the singular form.

23. "Are (there) included bed linens and table service?"
25. "Is it necessary to sign a lease?"
26. "For that you will have to speak . . ."
27. *Quais* is the plural of *qual,* what, which.
33. *Pena,* besides "pen" also means pain, sorrow, pity.
35. *Querer dizer* to mean. "What do you mean with that?"
36. *Escada de serviço* service stairway.
38. *Remodelados* or *reformados* remodeled.
41. "Can we see . . ."
43. *Venho* from the verb *vir,* "I come."
44. "For nothing. At your orders."

QUIZ 33

1. _____ (I come) *ver o apartamento.*

    a. *vem*
    b. *venho*
    c. *como*

2. *Aquêle que* _____ (is) *para alugar.*

    a. *ver*
    b. *êste*
    c. *está*

3. _____ (there are) *dois.*

    a. *tem (há)*
    b. *venho (vem)*
    c. *lá*

4. *Não tem* _____ (furniture).
   a. *andar*
   b. *banheiro*
   c. *mobília*

5. _____ (how many) *peças (divisões) têm?*
   a. *como*
   b. *quantas*
   c. *muitas*

6. *Dá para a* _____ (street)?
   a. *cozinha*
   b. *pátio*
   c. *rua*

7. _____ (also) *dá para o pátio?*
   a. *também*
   b. *outro*
   c. *rua*

8. _____ (what) *são as condições?*
   a. *quais*
   b. *quando*
   c. *onde*

9. *A senhora* _____ (will find) *tudo o que precisar.*
   a. *andar*
   b. *terá*
   c. *achará*

10. *O prédio é* _____ (very) *moderno.*
    a. *manhã*
    b. *muito*
    c. *mobiliado*

ANSWERS

1 b.; 2 c.; 3 a.; 4 c.; 5 b.; 6 c.; 7 a.; 8 a.; 9 c.; 10 b.

67. SOME COMMON VERBS

1. *Ter* "to have"

   a. I have, etc. (Do not use the forms in parentheses until you are sure of their proper usage.)

tenho	temos
(tens)	(tendes)
tem	têm

Tenho um belo jardim.	I have a pretty garden.
Não tenho nada.	I don't have anything.
O senhor tem?	Do you have it?
Não tenho.	I don't have (it).
Tenho tempo.	I have time.
Não tenho dinheiro.	I don't have any money.
Não tenho filhos.	I don't have any children.
Êle não tem amigos.	He doesn't have any friends.
Tenho fome. (Estou com fome.)[1]	I'm hungry.
Tenho sêde. (Estou com sêde.)	I'm thirsty.
Tenho sono. (Estou com sono.)	I'm sleepy.
Tenho frio. (Estou com frio.)	I'm cold.

   ---

   [1] In this section, the form in parentheses is usually more common in Brazil.

Tenho razão.	I'm right.
Êle não tem razão.	He's not right.
Êles não têm razão.	They're wrong.
O senhor tem um cachimbo?	Do you have a pipe?
Não tenho. Não fumo.	I don't have (any). I don't smoke.
A fazenda tem muitos animais?	Does the farm have many animals?
Tem. Tem gado, cavalos, e carneiros.	Yes, it has. It has cattle, horses, and sheep.
Tenho vinte anos.	I'm twenty years old.
Tenho dor de cabeça. (Estou com dor de cabeça.)	I have a headache.
Ela tem dor de dente. (Ela está com dor de dente or dentes.)	She has a toothache.
O que é que você tem?	What's the matter with you?
Não tenho nada.	Nothing's the matter with me.
Êles têm pressa. (Êles estão com pressa.)	They're in a hurry.
Elas não tiveram bom êxito.	They were not successful.
Tenha a bondade de avisar-me.	Please inform me.
Tenha cuidado.	Be careful.
O senhor tem a palavra.	You have the floor.
Tenho saudades de minha terra.	I long for my country.

| *Tenho sorte. (Estou com sorte.)* | I'm lucky. |
| *Não tem importância.* | It doesn't matter. |

b. *Ter que* or *ter de* translates our "to have to":

Tenho que ir hoje.	I have to go today.
O senhor tem que acreditar.	You have to believe.
Os meninos têm de brincar.	The children have to play.
Ela tem de indagar.	She has to inquire.

c. Do I Have It?

Eu tenho?	Do I have it?
O senhor tem?	Do you have it?
Êle tem?	Does he have it?
Ela tem?	Does she have it?
Nós temos?	Do we have it?
Os senhores têm?	Do you have it?
Êles (elas) têm?	Do they have it?

d. Don't I Have It?

Eu não tenho?	Don't I have it?
O senhor não tem?	Don't you have it?
Êle não tem?	Doesn't he have it?
Ela não tem?	Doesn't she have it?
Nós não temos?	Don't we have it?
Os senhores não têm?	Don't you have it?
Êles (elas) não têm?	Don't they have it?

QUIZ 34

| 1. *Não tenho dinheiro.* | 1. I have a headache. |
| 2. *Não tenho nada.* | 2. Don't you have it? |

3. *Êle não tem razão.*	3. I don't have it.
4. *Tenho sono.*	4. I'm cold.
5. *Êle tem?*	5. They're in a hurry.
6. *Eu não tenho.*	6. I don't have any money.
7. *Tenho fome.*	7. Does he have it?
8. *Tenho frio.*	8. He's not right.
9. *Tenho vinte anos.*	9. I'm thirsty.
10. *O senhor não tem?*	10. Be careful.
11. *Tenho que ir hoje.*	11. I don't have anything.
12. *Êles têm pressa.*	12. I'm sleepy.
13. *Tenho sêde.*	13. I'm hungry.
14. *Tenho dor de cabeça.*	14. I have to go today.
15. *Tenha cuidado.*	15. I'm twenty years old.

ANSWERS

1—6; 2—11; 3—8; 4—12; 5—7; 6—3; 7—13; 8—4;
9—15; 10—2; 11—14; 12—5; 13—9; 14—1; 15—10.

2. *Haver* "to have" (auxiliary verb)

hei	*havemos*
(hás)	*(haveis)*
há	*hão*

a. *Haver* is not used to translate "to have" in the sense of "to possess" (*ter* is used for this meaning). *Haver* is used with the past participle to form compound tenses, but *ter* has been replacing it in this use:

Hei (tenho) aprendido muito.	I have learned (been learning) very much.
Havia (tinha) esquecido.	I had forgotten.

b. *Haver* is used in expressions of time:

Há quanto tempo?	How long ago?
Há pouco tempo.	Not long ago.
Há muito tempo.	A long time ago.
Êles telefonaram há três horas.	They phoned three hours ago.
Há dois dias que não me falam.	They haven't spoken to me for two days.

c. The third person singular *há* means "there is" or "there are" (*tem* is often used in this sense, especially in Brazil):

Há muita gente aqui.	There are many people here.
Há uma festa amanhã.	There is a party tomorrow.
Há muitos estrangeiros nessa cidade.	There are many foreigners in that city.

Houve and *havia* mean "there was" or "there were":

Houve um incêndio.	There was a fire.
Havia muita gente quando cheguei.	There were many people when I arrived.

Haverá means "there will be":

Haverá outro govêrno.[1]	There will be another government.

d. *Haver de* indicates intention, expectation, or obligation:

---

[1] *governo* Ⓟ.

Havemos de encontrar-nos um dia no Brasil.	We'll meet some day in Brazil.
Hei de ir agora mesmo.	I have to go right now.

e. Other uses:

Haja o que houver.	Come what may.
Que há de nôvo?	What's new?
Não há de quê.	Not at all; you're welcome; don't mention it.

3. *Fazer* "to do," "make"

faço	fazemos
(fazes)	(fazeis)
faz	fazem

Que vai fazer?	What are you going to do?
Como se faz isto?	How do you do this?
Ela fêz[1] a cama.	She made the bed.

a. The third person singular of *fazer* is used in some expressions about the weather:

Faz bom tempo.	The weather is good.
Ontem fêz mau tempo.	Yesterday the weather was bad.
Aqui nunca faz frio.	It's never cold here.
Faz calor no verão?	Is it warm in the summer?

---

[1] *fez* Ⓟ.

b. *Fazer* is used at times instead of *haver* in expressions of time:

Faz tempo que êle não me fala.	He hasn't spoken to me for some time.
Faz três dias que não o vejo.	I haven't seen him for three days.

c. Other uses of *fazer:*

Agora vocês podem fazer perguntas.	Now you can ask questions.
Faça o favor de cobrir tudo.	Please cover everything.
É preciso fazer fila?	Is it necessary to stand in line?
Êle ainda não faz a barba.	He doesn't shave yet.
Quando nos vai fazer uma visita?	When are you going to visit us?
Não faz mal.	It doesn't matter.
Vamos fazer uma viagem no verão.	We're going to take a trip in the summer.
Êle fêz dezoito anos ontem.	He became eighteen years old yesterday.

QUIZ 35

1. *Há uma festa amanhã.*	1. Three hours ago.
2. *Que vai fazer?*	2. It's cold.
3. *Faz bom tempo.*	3. Come what may.
4. *Há dois dias que não me falam.*	4. She made the bed.
5. *Faça o favor.*	5. What are you going to do?

6. *Faz frio.*	6. Please.
7. *Haja o que houver.*	7. There is a party tomorrow.
8. *Ela fêz a cama.*	8. The weather is good.
9. *Como se faz isto?*	9. They haven't spoken to me for two days.
10. *Há três horas.*	10. How do you do this?

ANSWERS

1—7; 2—5; 3—8; 4—9; 5—6; 6—2; 7—3; 8—4;
9—10; 10—1.

LESSON 37

68. NÃO SOU DAQUI
I'M A STRANGER HERE

(I'm A Stranger Here)

1. **Boa tarde.**
   Good afternoon.

2. **Boa tarde. Em que posso servi-lo?**
   Good afternoon. What can I do for you?

3. **Podia me dar (dar-me) algumas informações?**
   Could you give me some information?

4. **Com muito prazer.**
   Gladly. ("With much pleasure.")

5. **Não conheço a cidade e não posso me orientar (orientar-me).**
   I don't know the city and I can't find my way around.

6. **(Pois), é muito simples.**
(Well), it's quite simple.

7. **É que eu não sou daqui.**
You see, I'm a stranger here.

8. **Nesse caso eu lhe mostro (mostro-lhe) a cidade.**
In that case I'll show you the town.

9. **Agradeço muito.**
I'm very grateful to you.

10. **Vê aquêle prédio grande na esquina?**
Do you see that large building on the corner?

11. **Aquêle da bandeira?**
The one with the flag?

12. **Precisamente. É o correio. Em frente dêle, do outro lado da rua . . .**
That's right. ("Exactly.") That's the post office. Opposite it, on the other side of the street . . .

13. **Onde?**
Where?

14. **Lá (Acolá Ⓟ). O senhor vê aquêle outro prédio com o relógio?**
Over there. Do you see that other building with the clock?

15. **Ah sim, vejo.**
Oh, yes, I see it.

16. **É a Prefeitura. (É a Câmara Municipal. Ⓟ)**
That's the City Hall.

17. **Vejo . . . A propósito, em que rua estamos?**
I see. . . . By the way, what street are we on?

18. Estamos na rua principal da cidade.
We're on the city's main street.

19. Onde fica o pôsto policial (a esquadra ℗)?
Where is the police station?

20. No fim da rua. Siga sempre em frente.
At the end of the street. Go straight ahead.

21. E se não acerto?
What if I don't find it?

22. Vai acertar. É um prédio grande com uma grade de ferro em redor . . . O senhor vê aquela loja?
You'll find it. It's a big building with an iron fence around it . . . Do you see that store?

23. Que loja? Aquela à direita?
Which store? The one on the right?

24. Sim, aquela que tem um globo verde na vitrina (montra).
Yes, the one with a green globe in the window.

25. É uma barbearia?
Is it a barbershop?

26. Não, é uma farmácia. Há um médico na casa ao lado. Tem o nome na porta.
No, it's a pharmacy. A doctor lives in the house next door.
("There's a doctor in the house at the side.") His name's on the door. ("He has the name on the door.")

27. Êle tem o consultório na mesma casa em que mora?
Does he have his office in his home? ("Does he

have the office in the same house in which he lives ['dwells']?")

28. Tem, mas pela manhã está no hospital.
Yes, he does, but in the morning he is at the hospital.

29. Onde é o hospital?
Where is the hospital?

30. O hospital fica a duas quadras (dois quarteirões) daqui, um pouco antes de chegar à rodovia (estrada).
The hospital is two blocks from here, just before ("a little before") you come to the highway.

31. Como posso voltar a (ao) meu hotel?
How can I get back to my hotel?

32. Venha aqui. O senhor está vendo, é lá perto do . . . (Venha aqui, o senhor está a ver, acolá perto do...)
Come over here. You see it there, next to the . . . .

33. . . . cinema.
. . . movie theatre.

34. Exato (Exacto Ⓟ).
That's right.

35. Já sei.
I know. ("I already know.")

36. Por que não compra um guia?
Why don't you buy a guidebook?

37. Boa idéia (ideia Ⓟ). Onde posso comprar (comprá-lo)?
Good idea. Where can I buy (one)?

38. **Na estação ou em qualquer banca (quiosque) de jornais.**
    In the station or at any newspaper stand.

39. **A estação é longe daqui?**
    Is the station far from here?

40. **A estação fica na Praça Mauá.**
    The station is on Mauá Square.

41. **Onde há uma banca (um quiosque) de jornais por aqui?**
    Where is there a newsstand near here?

42. **Há uma (um) na esquina.**
    There's one on the corner.

43. **Fico-lhe muito grato.**
    Thank you very much. ("I remain much obliged to you.")

44. **Não há de quê. Foi um prazer poder ser-lhe útil.**
    Don't mention it. ("There is nothing for which to be grateful.") I'm very glad to have been of some assistance. ("It was a pleasure to be able to be useful to you.")

45. **Tive muita sorte em encontrá-lo. O senhor conhece muito bem a cidade.**
    I was very lucky to meet you. You know the city very well.

46. **Não é de admirar. Sou o prefeito (administrador do conselho).**
    It's not surprising. I'm the mayor.

NOTES

Title: *Não sou daqui*. I'm a stranger. ("I'm not from here.")

2. "Good afternoon. In what can I serve you?" *Posso,* I can, from *poder* to be able.[1]
3. *Podia?* Could you?; from *poder*.[1] *Poderia* could also be used.
5. *Orientar-se* to orient oneself, to get one's bearings, to find one's way.
7. "It's that I'm not from here."
11. "That one of the flag?"
15. *Vejo*. I see; from *ver* to see.[1]
31. *Voltar* to return.
34. "Exactly."
44. *Foi*. It was; from *ser* to be.[1]
45. "I had much luck in meeting you."
46. *Não é de admirar*. ("It is not to cause surprise.") It's not surprising.

QUIZ 36

1. *É a* ____ (City Hall).

   a. *simples*
   b. *Prefeitura (Câmara Municipal Ⓟ)*
   c. *cidade*

2. *Eu lhe mostro a* ____ (city).

   a. *correio*
   b. *cidade*
   c. *caso*

---

[1] For these and other irregular verbs see section 43 of the grammar summary.

3. *Aquêle prédio grande na* ___ (corner).
   a. *esquina*
   b. *correio*
   c. *rua*

4. *É o* ___ (post office).
   a. *prédio*
   b. *correio*
   c. *Prefeitura (Câmara Municipal ℗)*

5. *O senhor vê aquela* ___ (store)?
   a. *direita*
   b. *loja*
   c. *barbearia*

6. *Há um* ___ (doctor) *na casa ao lado.*
   a. *médico*
   b. *farmácia*
   c. *nome*

7. *Tem o nome na* ___ (door).
   a. *mesma*
   b. *porta*
   c. *consultório*

8. *Êle tem o consultório na mesma* ___ (house) *em que mora?*
   a. *porta*
   b. *lado*
   c. *casa*

9. *Um pouco* ___ (before) *de chegar à rodovia.*
   a. *barbearia*

  b. *antes*
  c. *jornais*

10. *Onde* _____ (can I) *comprar?*
  a. *posso*
  b. *conheço*
  c. *vejo*

ANSWERS

1 b.; 2 b.; 3 a.; 4 b.; 5 b.; 6 a.; 7 b.; 8 c.; 9 b.; 10 a.

LESSON 38

69. CUMPRIMENTANDO UM VELHO AMIGO
GREETING AN OLD FRIEND

(Meeting an Old Friend)

1. **P¹: Onde está o senhor Guimarães? . . . É aquêle senhor que acaba de chegar.**
   P: Where is Mr. Guimarães?—the gentleman who just arrived.

2. **G: Êle entrou na sala de jantar.**
   G: He went into the dining room.

3. **P:** *(entrando na sala de jantar e olhando em redor de si)* **Ah! Você está aí! Como vai, meu caro João?**
   P: *(entering the dining room and looking around)* Ah, there you are! How are you, ("my dear") John?

---

¹ *P.* stands for *Pedro* "Peter"; *G.* for *o Gerente do hotel* "the hotel manager"; *J.* for *João* "John"; *M.* for *Maria* "Mary."

4. **J: Muito bem. E você, Pedro? Está bem?**
J: Fine. And how are you, Peter? ("And you, Peter? Are you well?")

5. **P: Você fêz boa viagem?**
P: Did you have a good trip?

6. **J: Estupenda!**
J: Wonderful!

7. **P: Olhe. Vou apresentá-lo à minha espôsa.[1]**
P: ("Look.") I'd like you to meet my wife.

8. **J: Terei muito prazer em conhecê-la.**
J: I'll be delighted to meet her.

9. **P: Maria, apresento-lhe (apresento-te) o meu velho amigo, João Guimarães.**
P: Mary, this is an old friend, John Guimarães.

10. **J: Tenho muito prazer em conhecê-la, senhora.**
J: I'm very glad to know you.

11. **M: O prazer é todo meu. (O prazer é meu.)**
M: I'm glad to know you.

12. **J: A senhora sabe que (o) Pedro e eu somos velhos amigos.**
J: You know that Peter and I are old friends.

13. **M: Eu sei! Não há dia em que não me fale do senhor (de si).**
M: Yes, I know. Not a day goes by without his speaking of you. ("There is not a day in which he does not speak to me about you.")

---

[1] esposa Ⓟ.

14. **J: É mesmo? (De verdade?)**
    J: Really?

15. **P: Você não sabe quanto prazer tenho em vê-lo de nôvo (em tornar a vê-lo).**
    P: You don't know how happy I am to see you again.

16. **J: Eu também. Você não mudou nada.**
    J: The same here. You haven't changed a bit.

17. **P: Você também não mudou nada. Está sempre jovem.**
    P: You haven't changed either. You still look as young as ever.

18. **M: (A) sua senhora gosta dos Estados Unidos?**
    M: How does your wife like the United States?

19. **J: Já está acostumada.**
    J: She's gotten used to it.

20. **M: Ouvi dizer que a vida em Nova Iorque é muito diferente da vida no Rio de Janeiro.**
    M: I understand that life in New York is quite different from life in Rio de Janeiro.

21. **J: Com efeito. Há muita coisa (muitas coisas) lá bem diferente.**
    J: It certainly is. Many things there are different.

22. **M: Por exemplo?**
    M: For example?

23. **J: Por exemplo, a senhora nunca pensaria em ir almoçar numa farmácia, não é verdade?**
    J: For example, you wouldn't think of going to a pharmacy for lunch, would you?

24. **M: Numa farmácia?**
M: A pharmacy?

25. **P: Que brincadeira é essa?**
P: What kind of joke is that?

26. **J: Não é brincadeira. Estou falando (a falar) sério.**
Lá, numa farmácia pode-se tomar o café da
manhã Ⓑ (o primeiro almoço Ⓟ) . . .
o almôço . . . o jantar . . .
J: It's not a joke at all. One can have breakfast in
a pharmacy, or lunch or dinner. . . .

27. **P: Por favor, não brinque.**
P: You're joking.

28. **M: Mas como o senhor sabe, aqui numa farmácia**
só se aviam (só aviam) receitas médicas e vendem
remédios.
M: But as you know, here pharmacies only fill
prescriptions and sell medicine.

29. **J: Mas lá, além de aviarem receitas, servem boas**
refeições, sorvete e refrescos.
J: But over there, in addition to good meals you
can have ice cream and refreshments.

30. **M: E fazem as refeições com tudo cheirando**
(a cheirar Ⓟ) a remédio?
M: And one eats there with the smell of medicine
all around?

31. **J: Não, nada disso. São estabelecimentos**
grandes e muito bem organizados, com ar
condicionado no verão e com aquecimento no
inverno. E repito, pode-se comer como em um

restaurante qualquer (como em qualquer restaurante).

J: Oh, nothing of the sort. They are large and well-organized establishments, with air conditioning in the summer and heat in the winter. And there, I repeat, you can eat as well as in any restaurant.

32. **P: Numa farmácia! Meu Deus! Não me faça rir.**

P: In a pharmacy! For heaven's sake! Don't make me laugh!

33. **J: Sim, numa farmácia. Mas lá a farmácia não tem êsse nome. Chama-se "drugstore."**

J: Yes, in a pharmacy. But over there it's not called a pharmacy; it's called a "drugstore."

34. **P: Compreendo. É farmácia mas não se chama farmácia. Então, se não se chama farmácia, não é farmácia.**

P: I understand. It's a pharmacy but they don't call it a pharmacy. Then, if it's not called a pharmacy, it's not a pharmacy.

35. **J: Pois bem, numa "drugstore" vendem selos, cartões (bilhetes) postais, charutos, cigarros, aparelhos elétricos,[1] brinquedos, livros e outras miudezas.**

J: Well, in a drugstore they sell stamps, postcards, cigars, cigarettes, electrical appliances, toys, books, and other odds and ends.

36. **P: Então é um bazar.**

P: Then it's a bazaar!

---

[1] **eléctricos** Ⓟ.

37. J: Não é; é uma "drugstore."
  J: No it's not; it's still a "drugstore."

38. P: Maravilhas dos Estados Unidos!
  P: The wonders of America!

NOTES

7. "Look. I am going to introduce you to my wife."
8. "I will (shall) have much pleasure in knowing her."
9. "Mary, I present to you my old friend, John Guimarães."
10. "I have much pleasure in knowing you, madam." *Conhecê-la* is the infinitive *conhecer* "to know" and the object *a* "you" *(fem.)* (see item 2 of section 20 of grammar summary).
11. "The pleasure is (all) mine."
15. "You don't know how much pleasure I have in seeing you again." *Vê-lo* is the infinitive *ver* "to see" and the object *o* "you" *(masc.)*.
16. "I also."
17. *Está sempre jovem.* "You are always young." *Ser jovem* means to be young; *estar jovem* here means to look young.
19. "She is already accustomed."
20. "I heard say that life in New York is very different from life in Rio de Janeiro."
21. *Muita coisa* is a singular form used here in the sense of a plural; the plural form *muitas coisas* can also be used.
23. *Não é verdade?* means "Isn't it the truth," but the translation will vary according to the nature of the question; here it is given as "would you?"
26. "It is not a joke. I am speaking seriously."

27. "Please. Don't joke."
28. "But as you know, here in a pharmacy they only fill medical prescriptions and sell medicines."
29. *Servem* they serve.
30. "And one eats his meals with everything smelling of medicine?"
31. *Nada disso* "nothing of that." *Com aquecimento* "with heat."
32. *Deus* is "God," but such expressions as *Meu Deus* are translated "For heaven's (goodness') sake," etc.
33. *Não tem êsse nome.* "(It) doesn't have that name."
37. "It's not; it's a 'drugstore.' "

QUIZ 37

1. ____ (where) *está o senhor Guimarães?*
   a. *como*
   b. *onde*
   c. *entrar*

2. *É aquêle senhor que acaba de* ____ (arrive).
   a. *chegar*
   b. *jantar*
   c. *lado*

3. *Vou apresentá-lo à minha* ____ (wife).
   a. *cidade*
   b. *sala*
   c. *espôsa*

4. *Terei muito prazer em* ____ (to know her).
   a. *espôsa*
   b. *vê-lo*
   c. *conhecê-la*

5. *Apresento-lhe (apresento-te) o meu velho* ____ (friend) *João.*
   a. *prazer*
   b. *também*
   c. *amigo*

6. *A senhora* ____ (know) *que somos velhos amigos.*
   a. *conhecer*
   b. *sabe*
   c. *dizer*

7. *Eu* ____ (know).
   a. *sei*
   b. *vejo*
   c. *tenho*

8. *Você não* ____ (changed) *nada.*
   a. *acostumada*
   b. *mudou*
   c. *tomar*

9. *Você está sempre* ____ (young).
   a. *jovem*
   b. *nada*
   c. *brincadeira*

10. *A* ____ (life) *em Nova Iorque é muito diferente.*
    a. *coisa*
    b. *vida*
    c. *rua*

11. *Há muita* ____ (thing) *lá bem diferente.*
    a. *vida*
    b. *receita*
    c. *coisa*

12. *Aqui* ____ (they sell) *remédios.*
    a. *servem*
    b. *vendem*
    c. *jantar*

13. *Servem* ____ (good) *refeições.*
    a. *boas*
    b. *distinta*
    c. *receitas*

14. *São estabelecimentos* ____ (large).
    a. *jovem*
    b. *grandes*
    c. *charutos*

15. *Com ar condicionado no* ____ (summer).
    a. *sempre*
    b. *verão*
    c. *nada*

16. *Com aquecimento no* ____ (winter).
    a. *inverno*
    b. *sorvete*
    c. *como*

17. ____ (it's called) *"drugstore."*
    a. *acostumada*
    b. *chama-se*
    c. *jantar*

18. *A farmácia não tem êsse* ____ (name).
    a. *refrescos*
    b. *tomar*
    c. *nome*

19. *Não me faça* ____ (laugh).
    a. *mas*
    b. *rir*
    c. *jantar*

20. *Numa "drugstore" vendem* ____ (books).
    a. *brinquedos*
    b. *livros*
    c. *refrescos*

ANSWERS

1 b.; 2 a.; 3 c.; 4 c.; 5 c.; 6 b.; 7 a.; 8 b.; 9 a.; 10 b.;
11 c.; 12 b.; 13 a.; 14 b.; 15 b.; 16 a.; 17 b.; 18 c.; 19 b.;
20 b.

70. THE COMMONEST VERBS AND THEIR COMMONEST FORMS

1. *Fazer* "to do," "make"

	PRESENT	PAST	FUTURE
I	*faço*	*fiz*	*farei*
You (sing.)	*(fazes)*	*(fizeste)*	*(farás)*
He, she, it	*faz*	*fêz*[1]	*fará*
We	*fazemos*	*fizemos*	*faremos*
You (pl.)	*(fazeis)*	*(fizestes)*	*(fareis)*
They	*fazem*	*fizeram*	*farão*

IMPERATIVE

Familiar:	Polite:
(Faze!) sing.	*Faça!* sing.
(Fazei!) pl.	*Façam!* pl.

---

[1] *fez* Ⓟ.

Eu mesmo o fiz.		I made (did) it myself.
Êles farão muitas promessas.		They will make many promises.
Ela o faz de algodão.		She is making it (out) of cotton.
Faça o mais cedo possível.		Do (it) as soon as possible.

2. *Haver* "to have" (auxiliary verb, usually replaced by *ter* today)

	PRESENT	PAST	FUTURE
I	*hei*	*houve*	*haverei*
You (sing.)	*(hás)*	*(houveste)*	*(haverás)*
He, she, it	*há*	*houve*	*haverá*
We	*havemos*	*houvemos*	*haveremos*
You (pl.)	*(haveis)*	*(houvestes)*	*(havereis)*
They	*hão*	*houveram*	*haverão*

IMPERATIVE

Familiar:	Polite:
(Há!) sing.	*Haja!* sing.
(Havei!) pl.	*Hajam!* pl.

Hei (tenho) colocado tudo no seu lugar.	I have put (been putting) everything in its place.
Não há estrêlas[2] no céu.	There are no stars in the sky.
Elas não haviam favorecido isso.	They (*fem.*) had not favored that.
Não houve guerra nesse ano.	There was no war that year.

[2] *estrelas* Ⓟ.

3. *Ir* "to go"

	PRESENT	PAST	FUTURE
I	*vou*	*fui*	*irei*
You (sing.)	*(vais)*	*(fôste)*[1]	*(irás)*
He, she, it	*vai*	*foi*	*irá*
We	*vamos*	*fomos*	*iremos*
You (pl.)	*(ides)*	*(fôstes)*[1]	*(ireis)*
They	*vão*	*foram*	*irão*

IMPERATIVE

Familiar:	Polite:
(Vai!) sing.	*Vá!* sing.
(Ide!) pl.	*Vão!* pl.

Vou ao Brasil no varão.	I am going to Brazil in the summer.
Êle vai sòzinho.	He's going by himself.
Eu vou jogar tênis[2] *amanhã.*	I'm going to play tennis tomorrow. (This contruction is often used to express future actions.)
Êle foi vê-la.	He went to see her.
Vamos!	Let's go!
Vá com ela.	Go with her.

4. *Vir* "to come"

	PRESENT	PAST	FUTURE
I	*venho*	*vim*	*virei*
You (sing.)	*(vens)*	*(vieste)*	*(virás)*
He, she, it	*vem*	*veio*	*virá*

---

[1] No accent mark in Portugal.

We	vimos	viemos	viremos
You (pl.)	(vindes)	(viestes)	(vireis)
They	vêm	vieram	virão

IMPERATIVE

Familiar: Polite:
(Vem!) sing.   Venha! sing.
(Vinde!) pl.   Venham! pl.

Vem comigo?	Are you coming with me?
Ninguém veio.	Nobody came.
Êles vêm todos os dias.	They come every day.
Ela virà ás duas horas.	She will come at two o'clock.
Venham comigo.	Come with me.

5. *Crer* "to believe"

	PRESENT	PAST	FUTURE
I	creio	cri	crerei
You (sing.)	(crês)	(crêste)[1]	(crerás)
He, she, it	crê	creu	crerá
We	cremos	cremos	creremos
You (pl.)	(credes)	(crêstes)[1]	(crereis)
They	crêem	creram	crerão

IMPERATIVE

Familiar: Polite:
(Crê!) sing.   Creia! sing.
(Crede!) pl.   Creiam! pl.

---

[1] No accent mark in Portugal.

Êle não crê em nada.   He doesn't believe in
                           anything.

6. *Dar* "to give"

	PRESENT	PAST	FUTURE
I	*dou*	*dei*	*darei*
You (sing.)	*(dás)*	*(deste)*	*(darás)*
He, she, it	*dá*	*deu*	*dará*
We	*damos*	*demos*	*daremos*
You (pl.)	*(dais)*	*(destes)*	*(dareis)*
They	*dão*	*deram*	*darão*

IMPERATIVE

Familiar:	Polite:
(Dá!) sing.	*Dê!* sing.
(Dai!) pl.	*Dêem!* pl.

Êle me deu essa   He gave me that lamp.
lâmpada.
Quando você vai me dar   When are you going to
resposta?   give me an answer?
Dê-lhe o título.   Give him the title.

7. *Ter* "to have"

	PRESENT	PAST	FUTURE
I	*tenho*	*tive*	*terei*
You (sing.)	*(tens)*	*(tiveste)*	*(terás)*
He, she, it	*tem*	*teve*	*terá*
We	*temos*	*tivemos*	*teremos*
You (pl.)	*(tendes)*	*(tivestes)*	*(tereis)*
They	*têm*	*tiveram*	*terão*

IMPERATIVE

Familiar:	Polite:
(Tem!) sing.	*Tenha!* sing.
(Tende!) pl.	*Tenham!* pl.

Ela tem muitos vestidos novos.	She has many new dresses.
Alguém tem que representar a escola.	Somebody has to represent the school.
Tiveram outra crise.	They had another crisis.
Tenha cuidado!	Be careful!

8. *Dizer* "to say"

	PRESENT	PAST	FUTURE
I	*digo*	*disse*	*direi*
You (sing.)	*(dizes)*	*(dissesste)*	*(dirás)*
He, she, it	*diz*	*disse*	*dirá*
We	*dizemos*	*dissemos*	*diremos*
You (pl.)	*(dizeis)*	*(dissestes)*	*(direis)*
They	*dizem*	*disseram*	*dirão*

IMPERATIVE

Familiar:	Polite:
(Dize!) sing.	*Diga!* sing.
(Dizei!) pl.	*Digam!* pl.

Dizem que êle tem muitas dívidas.	They say he has many debts.
Ela disse que tinha certas dúvidas.	She said she had certain doubts.

Que dirá ela amanhã?   What will she say
                             tomorrow? I wonder
                             what she will say
                             tomorrow.

Diga-me a verdade.   Tell me the truth.

9. *Pôr* "to put"

	PRESENT	PAST	FUTURE
I	*ponho*	*pus*	*porei*
You (sing.)	*(pões)*	*(puseste)*	*(porás)*
He, she, it	*põe*	*pôs*	*porá*
We	*pomos*	*pusemos*	*poremos*
You (pl.)	*(pondes)*	*(pusestes)*	*(poreis)*
They	*põem*	*puseram*	*porão*

IMPERATIVE

Familiar: Polite:
(Põe!) sing.   *Ponha!* sing.
(Ponde!) pl.   *Ponham!* pl.

Onde o senhor pôs as   Where did you put the
instruções?   instructions?
Ponha a lenha aqui.   Put the wood here.
Vamos pôr as revistas   We are going to put the
na mesa.   magazines on the
                                table.

Êle não porá nada na   He will not put anything
cadeira.   on the chair.

10. *Querer* "to wish," "to want"

	PRESENT	PAST	FUTURE
I	*quero*	*quis*	*quererei*
You (sing.)	*(queres)*	*(quiseste)*	*(quererás)*
He, she, it	*quer*	*quis*	*quererá*
We	*queremos*	*quisemos*	*quereremos*
You (pl.)	*(quereis)*	*(quisestes)*	*(querereis)*
They	*querem*	*quiseram*	*quererão*

IMPERATIVE

Familiar:	Polite:
(Quer! Quere!) sing.	*(Quiera!)* sing.
(Querei!) pl.	*Queiram!* pl.

| *Quero permanecer aqui.* | I want to stay here. |
| *Não quiseram perdoar-nos.* | They wouldn't (didn't want to) pardon us. |

11. *Trazer* "to bring"

	PRESENT	PAST	FUTURE
I	*trago*	*trouxe*[1]	*trarei*
You (sing.)	*(trazes)*	*(trouxeste)*	*(trarás)*
He, she, it	*traz*	*trouxe*	*trará*
We	*trazemos*	*trouxemos*	*traremos*
You (pl.)	*(trazeis)*	*(trouxestes)*	*(trareis)*
They	*trazem*	*trouxeram*	*trarão*

---

[1] In these forms *x* is pronounced like *s* in *see*.

IMPERATIVE

Familiar: Polite:
(Traze!) sing.   *Traga!* sing.
(Trazei!) pl.   *Tragam!* pl.

Que história triste nos   What sad story are you
  traz hoje?   bringing us today?
Êle viajou por Portugal   He traveled through
  mas não me trouxe   Portugal but he didn't
  nada.   bring me anything.
Traga para cá!   Bring it here!

12. *Sair* "to leave"

	PRESENT	PAST	FUTURE
I	*saio*	*saí*	*sairei*
You (sing.)	*(sais)*	*(saíste)*	*(sairás)*
He, she, it	*sai*	*saiu*	*sairá*
We	*saímos*	*saímos*	*sairemos*
You (pl.)	*(saís)*	*(saístes)*	*(saireis)*
They	*saem*	*saíram*	*sairão*

IMPERATIVE

Familiar: Polite:
(Saí!) sing.   *Saia!* sing.
(Sai!) pl.   *Saiam!* pl.

Saio agora.   I'm leaving now.
Ela saiu por aqui.   She went out this way.

13. *Ver* "to see"

	PRESENT	PAST	FUTURE
I	*vejo*	*vi*	*verei*
You (sing.)	*(vês)*	*(viste)*	*(verás)*
He, she, it	*vê*	*viu*	*verá*
We	*vemos*	*vimos*	*veremos*
You (pl.)	*(vêdes)*[1]	*(vistes)*	*(vereis)*
They	*vêem*	*viram*	*verão*

IMPERATIVE

Familiar:	Polite:
(Vê!) sing.	*Veja!* sing.
(Vêde!)[1] pl.	*Vejam!* pl.

Êle não vê bem sem os óculos.	He can't see well without his glasses.
Mas eu os vi ontem!	But I saw them yesterday!
O senhor verá que o que digo é verdade.	You'll see that what I say is true.

14. *Saber* "to know"

	PRESENT	PAST	FUTURE
I	*sei*	*soube*	*saberei*
You (sing.)	*(sabes)*	*(soubeste)*	*(saberás)*
He, she, it	*sabe*	*soube*	*saberá*
We	*sabemos*	*soubemos*	*saberemos*
You (pl.)	*(sabeis)*	*(soubestes)*	*(sabereis)*
They	*sabem*	*souberam*	*saberão*

---

[1] *Vede, vedes* Ⓟ.

IMPERATIVE

Familiar:	Polite:
(Sabe!) sing.	*Saiba!* sing.
(Sabei!) pl.	*Saibam!* pl.

Sei que a vida lá está cara.	I know that living there is expensive.
Eu soube o segrêdo[1] ontem.	I found out (learned) the secret yesterday.
Os senhores saberão o valor mais tarde.	You will know (find out) its value later.

15. *Poder* "to be able"

	PRESENT	PAST	FUTURE
I	*posso*	*pude*	*poderei*
You (sing.)	*(podes)*	*(pudeste)*	*(poderás)*
He, she, it	*pode*	*pôde*	*poderá*
We	*podemos*	*pudemos*	*poderemos*
You (pl.)	*(podeis)*	*(pudestes)*	*(podereis)*
They	*podem*	*puderam*	*poderão*

IMPERATIVE

Familiar:	Polite:
(Pode!) sing.	*Possa!* sing.
(Podei!) pl.	*Possam!* pl.

Não pode chover mais.	It can't rain any more.
Poderei escolher o melhor?	Will I be able to pick the best one?
Posso ligar agora?	Can I connect it (turn it on) now?

---

[1] *segredo* Ⓟ.

LESSON 39

71. WHAT'S IN A NAME?

(What's In A Name?)

Como se chama êle?
What's his name?

Êle se chama (chama-se) João Coutinho.
His name is João (John) Coutinho.

Como se chama a jovem que está com êle?
What's the name of the young lady with him?

Ela se chama Maria Campos. (Chama-se Maria Campos.)
Her name is Maria (Mary) Campos.

Como se chama o pai dela?
What's her father's name?

O pai dela se chama (chama-se) Carlos Campos.
His name is Carlos (Charles) Campos.

Mas eu o conheço (conheço-o)! Êle é juiz, não é?
Why, I know him! He's a judge, isn't he?

É. E você conhece a sua senhora (a senhora), Dona Ana?
That's right. Do you know his wife, Dona Ana?

Não conheço, mas (o) João Campos deve ser irmão dessa jovem.
I don't know her, but João (John) Campos must be that girl's brother.

Você está certo. (Tem razão.) Todos nós lhe

chamamos Joãozinho. E ela tem outro irmão, Chico.

That's right. We all call him Joãozinho (Johnny). And she has another brother, Chico.

Ah, sim! Francisco.

Of course! Francisco (Francis).

Mas mais interessante ainda é que (a) Maria tem duas irmãs, uma mais velha e a outra mais nova, e ambas são bonitas.

But even more interesting is the fact that Maria has two sisters, one older and one younger than she is, and both of them are pretty.

Não me diga! Como se chamam?

You don't say! What are their names?

A mais velha é Isabel Gomes, quer dizer, é casada. Casou com o General Gomes do exército.

The older one is Isabel Gomes, that is, she is married. She married General Gomes of the army.

O General Eduardo Gomes?

General Eduardo (Edward) Gomes?

Êsse mesmo.

That's right.

É meu tio. E a irmã mais nova?

He's my uncle. How about the younger sister?

(A) Teresinha? É uma beleza.

Theresa ("little Theresa")? She's a beauty.

Diga-me mais.

Tell me more.

Tem onze anos. E . . .
She's eleven years old. And . . .

Chega. Vamos tomar um cafèzinho.
That's enough. Let's go get some coffee.

NOTES

Chamar-se is a reflexive verb, literally "to call oneself."

eu me chamo	nós nos chamamos
(tu te chamas)	(vós vos chamais)
êle se chama	êles se chamam

See Lesson 15, part 10, and item 6 of section 19 of grammar summary.

Dona and the first name are often used to refer to a married woman. Thus, *a senhora Campos,* Mrs. Campos, would often be referred to by those who know her as *Dona Ana.* (In Portugal, *a Sra. D. Ana* is used.) *Dona* can also be used with unmarried and even young ladies.

Jovem refers to a young person, masculine or feminine; modifying words will make the reference clearer: *irmão dessa jovem* brother of that young girl; *irmão dêsse jovem* brother of that young man.

Você está certo. You are right.

Tem razão. You are right.

Não me diga! ("Don't tell me!") You don't say!

Ésse mesmo the same one

E a irmã mais nova? And the younger sister?

LESSON 40

72. PORTUGUESE IN A LIGHTER VEIN

(Portuguese In A Lighter Vein)

UMA PERDA DE POUCA IMPORTÂNCIA
A Minor Loss

—Tenha a bondade de me dar (dar-me) "A Liberdade." Não tenho trôco.[1] Pode trocar esta nota?

—O senhor me paga (O senhor paga) amanhã—diz
a vendedora.

—E se eu morrer esta noite?

—Ora! A perda não seria grande.

"Please give me a copy of *Liberty*. I haven't any
change. Can you change this bill?"

"You can pay me tomorrow," says the vendor.

"What if I should die tonight?"

"Oh, it wouldn't be a great loss."

UMA LIÇÃO DE ETIQUETA
A Lesson in Etiquette

Pedro e João vão a um restaurante para jantar.
Ambos pedem um bife. O garçom Ⓑ (empregado Ⓟ)
os serve (serve-lhos). Quando Pedro tira para si o
maior bife (bife maior), João, zangado, lhe diz (diz-lhe):

---

[1] Notice how Portuguese punctuation in dialogues differs
from English: (1) There are no quotation marks and (2) each
change of speaker is indicated by a dash (see item 1 of section
4 of grammar summary).

Que maneiras (que) você tem! Foi o primeiro a se servir (servir-se) e tirou o maior.

Pedro responde:

—Se você estivesse em (no) meu lugar, qual teria tirado?

—O menor (mais pequeno), naturalmente.

—Então, por que se queixa? Não o tem aí?

Peter and John go to a restaurant for dinner. They both order steak. The waiter serves them. When Peter grabs the bigger steak, John says to him angrily:

"What bad manners you have! You helped yourself first and you took the bigger piece."

Peter answers:

"If you had been in my place, which would you have taken?"

"The smaller one, of course."

"Then what are you complaining about? You have it, don't you?"

NOTES

Perda loss.

De pouca importância of little importance.

Tenha a bondade. Please. ("Have the kindness.")

O senhor (me) paga amanhã. "You pay (me) tomorrow."

E se eu morrer esta noite? And if I die tonight? *Morrer* is a form of the future subjunctive (see items 1 and 5 of section 31 of grammar summary).

A perda não seria grande. The loss would not be great. *Seria* is the conditional of the verb *ser* (see section 33 of grammar summary).

Jantar to have dinner; dinner.

Pedem they ask for; from *pedir* to ask for.

Foi o primeiro a se servir (servir-se) "You were the first
in serving himself."
Se você estivesse em (no) meu lugar, qual teria tirado?
"If you had been in my place, which would you
have taken?" *Estivesse* is the imperfect subjunctive
of *estar* to be (see item 1, section 31 of grammar
summary, and item 3, section 34 of grammar
summary). *Terra tirado* is the perfect conditional of
tirar to take (see item 3, section 33 of the grammar
summary).
Então, por que se queixa? Não o tem aí? Then, why
do you complain? Don't you have it there?

UM OTIMISTA[1]
An Optimist

O chefe duma firma comercial importante, olhando
(para) uma fórmula de pedido de emprêgo,[2] fica surprêso (surpreendido) ao notar que o candidato ao
cargo que (ao notar que o candidato), carecia de experiência, pede (e pedia) um ordenado excessivo.

—Não acha—perguntou perplexo,—que está pedindo
(está a pedir um) excessivo ordenado em vista da sua
pouca experiência?

—Pelo contrário—respondeu o pretendente,—um
trabalho do qual não se sabe absolutamente nada é
mais difícil e deve merecer um pagamento melhor.

The head of an important firm, looking at an application, is astonished on noticing that the applicant for
the position, although lacking experience, is asking for
an excessive salary.

---

[1] optimista Ⓟ.
[2] emprego Ⓟ.

Rather puzzled, he asks him: "Don't you think you're asking for too high a salary, considering the little experience you have?"

"On the contrary," replies the applicant. "Work which one knows nothing about is more difficult and should be better paid."

NOTES

Olhando looking; from *olhar* to look.

Fica surprêso (surpreendido) is ("remains") surprised, astonished.

Não acha? Don't you think? *Achar* to find, also has taken on the meaning of to believe, to think.

Respondeu and *perguntou* are past tense forms of *responder* and *perguntar*.

O ESPÍRITO PRÁTICO
The Practical Mind

Um comerciante apareceu um dia na casa dum fazendeiro (lavrador) e pediu um quilo de manteiga. O fazendeiro (lavrador) respondeu que trocaria êsse quilo de manteiga por um par de meias de lã.

Quando o comerciante contou o fato[1] à mulher (à sua esposa), ela propôs o seguinte:

—Temos uma colcha de lã; eu a desfaço (desfaço-a) e dela farei um par de meias.

Assim fêz, e o comerciante deu o par de meias e recebeu um quilo de manteiga. Desde então, quando o comerciante precisava de manteiga, (a) sua mulher desfazia um pouco da colcha e tricotava umas meias.

---

[1] facto Ⓟ.

Mas chegou um dia em que só tinha lã para uma única meia. O comerciante a levou (levou-a) ao fazendeiro (lavrador), pedindo meio quilo de manteiga.

—Não—respondeu o fazendeiro (lavrador)—, dou-lhe um quilo. (A) minha mulher desfaz as meias para uma colcha que está fazendo (a fazer). Só precisa desta meia para acabá-la.

A merchant went to the house of a farmer and asked him for a kilogram of butter. The farmer answered that he would exchange it for a pair of woolen socks.

When the merchant told his wife about it, she proposed: "We have a woolen quilt; I'll unravel it and I'll make a pair of socks."

She did so and the merchant gave the pair of socks in exchange for the kilogram of butter. From then on, when the merchant needed butter, his wife unraveled some of the quilt and knitted some socks. But one day she had just enough wool for one sock. The merchant took it to the farmer and asked him for half a kilogram of butter.

"No," said the farmer, "I'll give you a kilogram. My wife unravels the socks for a quilt she is making. All she needs is this one sock to finish it."

NOTES

O espírito the spirit, mind.
Trocaria he would exchange; from *trocar* to exchange, change.
Propôs she proposed; from *propor* to propose, suggest.
Desfaço I'll unravel; from *desfazer* to unravel, undo.
Farei I'll make; from *fazer* to make, to do.

Levou he took; from *levar* to take (away, along).
Um pouco de a little of.
Tinha she had; from *ter* to have.
Pedindo asking; from *pedir* to ask (for).
Dou I'll give; from *dar* to give.
Acabá-la to finish it; a combination of *acabar* to finish, and *a* it, referring to the quilt.

73. IMPORTANT SIGNS

Homens or *Cavalheiros*	Men
Senhoras or *Damas*	Women
Lavatório	Lavatory
Fechado	Closed
Aberto	Open
É proibido fumar	No Smoking
É proibido entrar	No Admittance
Bata	Knock
Toque a campainha	Ring
Alto!	Stop!
Curva	Curve
Pare!	Stop!
Siga!	Go!
Cuidado! Atenção!	Look Out! Attention!
Perigo!	Danger!
Devagar!	Slow!
Desvio	Detour
Cautela!	Caution!
Conserve a sua direita.	Keep to the Right.
Siga pela direita	Keep to the Right
Ponte	Bridge
É proibido estacionar	No Parking

Vestiário	Check Room
Câmbio	(Money) Exchange
Informações	Information
Sala de espera	Waiting Room
É proibido debruçar-se	Don't Lean Out (of the window)
Vagão	Freight Car
Ferrovia	Railroad
Expresso or *Rápido*	Express
Parada (Paragem Ⓟ)	Stop (bus, streetcar, etc.)
É proibido colocar or *pregar* or *afixar (x=ks) cartazes*	Post No Bills
Em consêrto[1]	Under Repair
Caixa (x=sh)	Cashier
Entrada	Entrance
Saída	Exit
Quartos mobiliados (mobilados)	Furnished Rooms
Apartamentos	Apartments
Tinta fresca	Wet Paint
Encruzilhada	Crossroads
Açougue	Butcher Shop
Padaria	Bakery
Leiteria	Dairy
Alfaiataria	Tailor's Shop
Sapataria	Shoe Store
Barbearia	Barbershop
Empório Ⓑ, *Mercearia*	Grocery Store
Farmácia	Pharmacy
Confeitaria	Confectionery
Papelaria	Stationery Store

---

[1] *conserto* Ⓟ.

Caixa postal	Letter Box
Café e Bar	Tavern, Bar
Delegacia de polícia	Police Station
Pôsto policial	Police Station
(esquadra Ⓟ*)*	
Vinhos	Wines
Pôsto[1] de gasolina	Gas Station
Livraria	Bookstore
Prefeitura (Câmara	City Hall
Municipal Ⓟ*)*	
(Água) Fria	Cold (water)
(Água) Quente	Hot (water)

QUIZ 38

1. Entrada	1. No Smoking
2. Desvio	2. Express
3. Devagar!	3. No Parking
4. Fechado	4. Open
5. Aberto	5. Exit
6. É proibido fumar	6. Stop!
7. Expresso	7. Detour
8. É proibido estacionar	8. Entrance
9. Saída	9. Closed
10. Pare!	10. Slow!

ANSWERS

1—8; 2—7; 3—10; 4—9; 5—4; 6—1; 7—2; 8—3;
9—5; 10—6.

---

[1] *Pôsto* Ⓟ.

FINAL QUIZ

When you get 100% on this Quiz you can consider that you have mastered the course.

1. *Faça o favor de* _____ (tell me) *onde é a estação.*
   a. *diga-me*
   b. *me dizer (dizer-me)*
   c. *me trazer (trazer-me)*

2. _____ (can) *o senhor me dizer (dizer-me) onde é o correio?*
   a. *pode*
   b. *tem*
   c. *custa*

3. *Onde* _____ (is there) *um bom restaurante?*
   a. *faz*
   b. *há*
   c. *hoje*

4. _____ (bring me) *um pouco de pão.*
   a. *conhecê-la*
   b. *servi-lo*
   c. *traga-me*

5. _____ (I need) *presunto.*
   a. *preciso de*
   b. *tem*
   c. *ninguém*

6. _____ (I would like) *um pouco mais de carne.*
   a. *traga-me*
   b. *preciso de*
   c. *gostaria de*

7. *Vou* ____ (to introduce you) *a meu amigo.*
   a. *apresentá-lo*
   b. *o prazer*
   c. *vê-lo*

8. *Onde* ____ (is) *o livro?*
   a. *está*
   b. *és*
   c. *êste*

9. *Tenha* ____ (the goodness) *de falar mais devagar.*
   a. *a bondade*
   b. *o favor*
   c. *o prazer*

10. ____ (we speak) *português.*
    a. *falam*
    b. *ficamos*
    c. *falamos*

11. ____ (Go) *lá.*
    a. *vá*
    b. *fale*
    c. *venho*

12. ____ (Come) *cá.*
    a. *venha*
    b. *comigo*
    c. *vamos*

13. *Como se* ____ (call) *o senhor?*
    a. *charuto*
    b. *chama*
    c. *chover*

14. *Que dia da* ____ *(week)* *é hoje?*
    a. *semana*
    b. *mês*
    c. *ano*

15. *Que* ____ *(time)* *são?*
    a. *horas*
    b. *agora*
    c. *tempo*

16. *Não* ____ *(I have)* *cigarros.*
    a. *tempo*
    b. *tenho*
    c. *ter*

17. *O senhor* ____ *(don't want)* *carne?*
    a. *não fica*
    b. *não compra*
    c. *não quer*

18. ____ *(Please)* *de escrever o nome aqui.*
    a. *comprar*
    b. *faça o favor*
    c. *por certo*

19. ____ *(There were)* *muitos livros na livraria.*
    a. *há*
    b. *havia*
    c. *lá*

20. ____ *(I prefer)* *esta.*
    a. *prefiro*
    b. *prefere*
    c. *prefira*

21. *Vamos* ____ (to have dinner).
   a. *jantar*
   b. *almoçar*
   c. *mostrar*

22. *São* ____ (2:15).
   a. *duas e meia*
   b. *duas e quinze*
   c. *duas e cinco*

23. *Venha* ____ (tomorrow morning).
   a. *ontem pela manhã*
   b. *amanhã pela manhã*
   c. *amanhã ao meio-dia*

24. *Em que* ____ (can I) *servi-lo?*
   a. *pode*
   b. *chamo*
   c. *posso*

25. *Não* ____ (has) *importância.*
   a. *tenha*
   b. *tem*
   c. *houve*

ANSWERS

1 b.; 2 a.; 3 b.; 4 c.; 5 a.; 6 c.; 7 a.; 8 a.; 9 a.; 10 c.;
11 a.; 12 a.; 13 b.; 14 a.; 15 a.; 16 b.; 17 c.; 18 b.; 19 b.;
20 a.; 21 a.; 22 b.; 23 b.; 24 c.; 25 b.

SUMMARY OF
PORTUGUESE GRAMMAR

1. THE ALPHABET

Letter	Name	Letter	Name	Letter	Name
a	a	i	i	r	erre
b	bê	j	jota	s	esse
c	cê	l	ele	t	tê
d	dê	m	eme	u	u
e	é	n	ene	v	vê
f	efe	o	ó	x	xis
g	gê	p	pê	z	zê
h	agá	q	quê		

2. PRONUNCIATION

SIMPLE VOWELS[1]

a (1) in a stressed position it is "open" as in *ah* or *father*.

   (2) in unstressed positions and in the case of the article *a* and its plural *as* ("the") it tends to be more "closed" like the final *a* in *America* (this is particularly true in Portugal and in general with unstressed final *a*).

e (1) "open" as in *best; é* has this sound.

   (2) "closed" somewhat between the sound of *a* in *case* and *e* in *fez; ê* has this sound; so does nasal *e*.

---

[1] Also see Lessons 1 and 3 of Conversation Manual.

(3) variations occur in different areas:

    a. in a final unstressed position: in Brazil it varies between the sound of *i* in *did* and the *i* in *machine;* in Portugal it is often clipped sharply, being like a mute *e,* or it is dropped.

    b. stressed *e* before *j, ch, lh, nh,* in Portugal can have the sound of final *a* in *America,* or of closed *e.*

    c. in an unstressed position it is sometimes pronounced as *e* in *be,* in parts of Brazil, as mute *e* in Portugal, or as *i* in *did* in both.

i as *i* in *machine.*

o (1) "open" as *o* in *off;* ó has this sound.

    (2) "closed" as in *rose;* ô has this sound and so does nasal *o.*

    (3) in an unstressed position and in the case of the definite article *o, os* ("the") it is also pronounced like *oo* in *boot;* this is heard quite regularly in Portugal, but less consistently in Brazil.

u approximates *u* in *rule.*

VOWEL COMBINATIONS[1]

ai   *ai* in *aisle.*

au   *ou* in *out.*

ei   *ey* in *they.*

---

[1] Also see Lesson 4.

éi   similar sound with open *e*. [1]

eu   *ey* of *they* plus *u* of *lute*.

éu   similar but with open *e*.

ia   *ya* in *yard*.

ié   *ye* in *yes*.

ie   similar but with close *e*.

io   *yo* in *yoke*.

iu   *e* plus *u* of *lute*.

oi   *oy* in *boy*.

ói   similar but with open *o*.

ou   *ou* in *soul*.

ua   *wah,* as *ua* in *quadrangle*.

ué   *we* in *wet*.

ui   *we* (if main stress is on *u*, however, like *u* of *lute* plus *e*).

uo   *wo* in *woe,* or as *uó*.

CONSONANTS [2]

Those consonants not mentioned are approximately like English.

c   before *a, o,* and *u,* and before another consonant like *c* in *cut*.

c   before *e* and *i* like *c* in *center*.

ch   this combination as *ch* in *machine*.

---

[1] The sound indicated in **éi** may also be given in the case of **ei** in some cases. This is also true of other members of the pairs given.

[2] Also see Lessons 1, 2, 3.

d	as *d* in *dog;* it is pronounced forcefully in Rio de Janeiro and with some speakers (especially before *e* or *i*) it approximates the *j* in *just.*
g	before *e* and *i* is somewhat like *s* in *measure.*
g	otherwise like *g* in *go.*
h	is not pronounced.
j	is like *g* before *e* and *i* (see above).
l	is formed with the tongue forward, the tip near the upper teeth.
l	in final position is quite soft.
lh	this combination is like *lli* in *million.*
m	in initial position in a word or syllable is like English *m;* in final position in a syllable or word it tends to nasalize the preceding vowel; this nasal quality is especially strong in Brazil, but it may be slight or even absent in Continental Portuguese. (Lips should not be closed in pronouncing *m* at the end of a word.)[1]
n	in initial position is like English *n;* in final position as for *m,* above.[1]
nh	as *ni* in *onion.*[1]
qu	before *a* or *o* is like *qu* in *quota.*
qu	before *e* or *i* is usually like *k.*
r	is pronounced by tapping the tip of the tongue against the gum ridge back of the upper teeth; initial *r* and *rr* are trilled with the tongue vibrating in this position; this

[1] Also see Lesson 4.

pronunciation is heard in Portugal and in
São Paulo. In Rio de Janeiro and in some
other parts of Brazil *r* is pronounced back
in the mouth (similar to a French back *r*).

s   between vowels is *z,* as *s* in *rose.*

s   before a voiced consonant (a consonant
sound produced with a vibration of the
cords, as *b, d, ge, gi, j, l, m, n, r, v, z*) tends
to be as *z* in *azure.*

s   before a voiceless consonant (a consonant
sound produced without a vibration of the
vocal cords, as hard *c* and hard *g, f, p, qu, t*),
and final *s* are pronounced as *s* in *see* in São
Paulo and by some *cariocas,* and as *sh* in
shine in Portugal and by some *cariocas.*

s   in initial position, or after a consonant, as
s in *see.*

ss   as *ss* in *passage.*

t   is much like English *t;* before *e* or *i* it is pronounced very forcefully by some *cariocas,*
being palatalized and approximating the *ch*
in *church.*

x   like *z* in some words: *exame;* like *sh* in some
words: *caixa;* like *s* in *see* in some words:
máximo; like *x* in *wax* in some words: *táxi.*

z   is generally like *z* in *zeal;* however, in final
position or before a voiceless consonant *s*
is also heard in Brazil, *sh* is the common pronunciation in Portugal and is also used by
some *cariocas;* before a voiced consonant it
is like *z* in *azure* in Portugal and with some
cariocas.

3. STRESS

1. Words ending in *a, e,* or *o* (or in one of these vowels and *s, m,* or *ns*) are stressed on the next to the last syllable:

   casa   house

2. Words ending in any letter, in a nasal vowel or diphthong (two vowels pronounced in union) are stressed on the last syllable:

   papel   paper
   manhã   morning
   descansei   I rested

3. Words not following the above rules have a written accent mark which indicates the stressed syllable:

   café   coffee

4. PUNCTUATION

In general, Portuguese punctuation is similar to English. Some differences are:

1. The dash is used in dialogues to indicate the words of the speakers:

—*Como vai o senhor?*
—*Muito bem, obrigado.*

2. Capitals are not used as frequently as in English. They are not used with adjectives of nationality, the days of the week and the months (except that in Portugal the months and the seasons are capitalized), nor is the pronoun *eu* ("I") capitalized:

Êles¹ são russos.	They are Russians.
Ela chegará na quinta.	She will arrive on Thursday.
Comprei o tapête² em setembro (Setembro ℗).	I bought the carpet in September.

3. Suspension points (. . .) are used more frequently than in English to indicate interruption, etc.

4. Notice the variance from English in the use of the decimal point:

3.000.000 de habitantes	3,000,000 inhabitants
5.289 metros	5,289 meters
Cr$ 8.300,00	8,300 cruzeiros
1.800$00	1,800 escudos (Portugal)

5. SOME ORTHOGRAPHIC SIGNS

1. The tilde (*til*) (˜) over a vowel indicates a nasal sound:

   posição   position

2. The dieresis (*trema*) (¨) is used in Brazil but not in Portugal in modern spelling over the letter *u* when it occurs after *q* or *g* and before *e* or *i* and is pronounced:

   eloqüente   eloquent
      (*eloquente* ℗)

---

¹ *eles, ele* ℗.
² *tapete* ℗.

3. The cedilla (*cedilha*) is used with *c* (ç) when it is pronounced *s* before *a, o,* or *u:*

    pedaço   piece, bit

4. Written accent marks are used to indicate the stressed syllable in words not following the regular rules (see GS3).[1] They also help distinguish between words spelled alike but with different meanings and between different forms of the same verb:

pôr to put   *por* for, by
pôde he was able, could   *pode* he is able, can

If one of the words is a form of the verb, often the first singular of the present indicative, it usually has an open vowel in the stem and the other word, often a noun, a closed vowel; Brazil uses an accent mark on the second form, but Portugal does not:

gosto I like   *gôsto (gosto* Ⓟ*)* taste

The circumflex accent (*acento circunflexo*) (ˆ) is used over stressed closed *e* and *o;* the acute accent (*acento agudo*) (´) is used over stressed open *a, e,* and *o:*

pára it stops   *para* for, to
avô grandfather   *avó* grandmother
célebre famous   *fé* faith

The acute accent is used over stressed *i* or *u* which do not combine with the preceding vowel:

país country   *pais* parents
saúde health   *saída* departure

---

[1] Refers to section 3 of the grammar summary.

The grave accent (*acento grave*) (`) replaces the acute accent in longer derived forms:

café coffee   *cafèzinho* small cup of
                                coffee (usually black)

The grave accent indicates a combination of *a* and a word beginning with *a* (demonstratives, as *aquêle*,[1] etc.) or with the definite article *a:*

àqueles to those   *à* to the

6. SYLLABLE DIVISION

1. A single consonant goes with the following vowel:

a-fi-nal   finally

2. Two consonants usually split:

in-ter-rom-per   to interrupt

  a. *ch, lh, nh* do not split:

bor-ra-cha   rubber, eraser
o-re-lha   ear
so-nhar   to dream

3. Two vowels which are pronounced separately are split:

vi-ú-va   widow
ca-ir   to fall
vo-ar   to fly

---

[1] *aquele* Ⓟ.

7. THE DEFINITE ARTICLE

	SINGULAR	PLURAL
Masculine	*o*	*os*
Feminine	*a*	*as*

SINGULAR

o menino	the boy
a menina	the girl

PLURAL

os meninos	the boys
as meninas	the girls

1. The definite article is also used:

    a. with abstract nouns:

A verdade vale mais que o dinheiro.	Truth is worth more than money.

    b. with nouns used in a general sense:

A mulher brasileira veste (-se) bem.	Brazilian women dress well.
As mulheres americanas vestem (-se) bem.	American women dress well.
O óleo é muito útil.	Oil is very useful.

    c. with the names of languages (except when immediately after *falar, de,* or *em;* the article is often not used with languages in some situations):

O português é fácil.	Portuguese is easy.
Falo inglês.	I speak English.
Tenho um livro de espanhol.	I have a Spanish book.

d. with expressions of time:

a semana passada	last week
às duas horas	at two o'clock

e. with days of the week:

na segunda-feira	on Monday

f. with the seasons:

a primavera	spring
(Primavera Ⓟ*)*	

g. with the names of most countries (but not with Portugal) and with other geographical names:

o Brasil	Brazil
a Itália	Italy
a África	Africa

h. with first names at times:

o Carlos	Charles

i. with titles or other words modifying a proper noun:

Êle jantou com o professor Silva.	He dined with Professor Silva.
O senhor Ramos não está em casa.	Mr. Ramos is not home.

j. with possessive pronouns and adjectives (Brazil uses the article less with possessive adjectives than does Portugal):

Êste¹ não é (o) meu lenço; é o seu.	This is not my handkerchief; it's yours.

---

¹ *este* Ⓟ.

k. with parts of the body and articles of clothing instead of the possessive form:

O menino lavou as mãos.	The boy washed his hands.
Ela perdeu as luvas.	She lost her gloves.

8. THE INDEFINITE ARTICLE

	SINGULAR	PLURAL
Masculine	*um*	*uns*
Feminine	*uma*	*umas*

SINGULAR

um homem	a man
uma mulher	a woman

PLURAL

uns homens	some (a few) men
umas mulheres	some (a few) women

1. The indefinite article is omitted:

a. before a noun of occupation, nationality, etc., coming after the verb, especially if the noun is not modified:

Êle é capitão.	He is a captain.
Ela é aluna.	She is a student.

b. before *cem* a hundred, and *mil* a thousand:

cem entrevistas	a hundred interviews
mil esperanças	a thousand hopes

c. in certain expressions:

Êle saiu sem chapéu.	He left without a hat.

9. CONTRACTIONS

1. $de + o = do$ $de + os = dos$ of the, from the
   $de + a = da$ $de + as = das$

   $a + o = ao$ $a + os = aos$ to the
   $a + a = à$ $a + as = às$

   $em + o = no$ $em + os = nos$ in the, on the
   $em + a = na$ $em + as = nas$

do menino	dos meninos	of the boy, of the boys
da menina	das meninas	of the girls, of the girls
ao menino	aos meninos	to the boy, to the boys
à menina	às meninas	to the girl, to the girls
no lago	nos lagos	in (on) the lake, in the lakes
na pátria	nas pátrias	in the fatherland, in the fatherlands

2. Contractions of *de* and *em* with the indefinite article (*um* and its other forms) are optional, both contracted and noncontracted forms being used:

de um artigo or dum artigo	of an article
de uma árvore or duma árvore	of a tree
em umas aldeias or numas aldeias	in some villages

De and *em* combine with the demonstrative forms (see GS25):

daquela	of that one
naquele	in that one

3. The preposition *a* combines with the initial *a* of demonstratives *aquêle*,[1] etc. and with the definite article *a:*

àquela	to that one
à baía	to the bay

10. DAYS OF THE WEEK

1. The days of the week are not capitalized. Saturday and Sunday are masculine; the other days are feminine. The article is generally used except after *ser:*

segunda-feira or *segunda*	Monday
têrça-feira or *têrça*[1]	Tuesday
quarta-feira or *quarta*	Wednesday
quinta-feira or *quinta*	Thursday
sexta-feira or *sexta*	Friday
sábado	Saturday
domingo	Sunday

Vou vê-lo na segunda.	I am going to see him Monday.
Hoje é têrça.	Today is Tuesday.

2. "On Monday," "on Mondays," etc.:

na segunda-feira	on Monday
nas segundas-feiras	on Mondays

---

[1] *aquele* Ⓟ.

11. THE NAMES OF THE MONTHS

The names of the months are masculine and usually are not capitalized in Brazil (but they are in Portugal: *Janeiro,* etc.). They are usually used without the definite article:

janeiro	January
fevereiro	February
março	March
abril	April
maio	May
junho	June
julho	July
agôsto (Agosto Ⓟ*)*	August
setembro	September
outubro	October
novembro	November
dezembro	December

12. THE NAMES OF THE SEASONS

a primavera	spring
o verão	summer
o outono	autumn
o inverno	winter

The names of the seasons are usually not capitalized in Brazil (but they are in Portugal). They are usually used with the definite article:

Ninguém vai lá no inverno. (Inverno Ⓟ*)*	Nobody goes there in (the) winter.

---

¹ *terça-feira, terça* Ⓟ.

13. MASCULINE AND FEMININE

Nouns referring to males are masculine; nouns referring to females are feminine:

o pai	the father	*a mãe*	the mother
o filho	the son	*a filha*	the daughter
o homem	the man	*a mulher*	the woman
o leão	the lion	*a leoa*	the lioness

The masculine plural of certain nouns can include both genders:

os pais	the parents, the father and mother
os irmãos	the brothers, the brother and sister, the brothers and sisters

---

MASCULINE NOUNS

1. Nouns ending in diphthongs (vowel combinations pronounced together), *m* (but not *em*), *s* and *o* are usually masculine:

o grau	the degree
o elogio	the praise
o dom	the gift
o lápis	the pencil
um abraço	an embrace, hug

2. Names of months, seas, rivers, mountains, letters of the alphabet are generally masculine:

Janeiro é o primeiro mês.	January is the first month.
o Atlântico	the Atlantic
o Amazonas	the Amazon (River)
o dê	the "d"

FEMININE NOUNS

1. Nouns ending in *a, ie, em, ade, ede,* and *ice* are usually feminine:

a bôca[1]	the mouth
a ordem	the order
a amizade	friendship
a parede	the wall
a velhice	old age

Common exceptions:

o homem	the man

a good number of words ending in *a,* especially *ma,* are masculine:

o drama	the drama
o clima	the climate
o dia	the day
o mapa	the map
o idioma	the language

2. Names of cities, towns, islands, and continents are usually feminine:

a Lisboa	Lisbon
a Sicília	Sicily
a América	America

Some exceptions:

o Rio de Janeiro	Rio de Janeiro
São Paulo	São Paulo
o Pôrto (Porto Ⓟ*)*	Porto

---

[1] *boca* Ⓟ.

14. THE PLURAL

1. Nouns ending in a vowel, including nasal vowels, or in a diphthong, usually add *s* to form the plural:

um ato[1]	one act	*dois atos*[1]	two acts
a maçã	the apple	*as maçãs*	the apples
a lei	the law	*as leis*	the laws

2. Feminine words ending in *ão* usually end in *ões* in the plural:

a ambição	ambition	*as ambições*	ambitions

3. Masculine words ending in *ão* usually end in *ões* in the plural:

o cartão	card	*os cartões*	cards

However, some end in *ãos* or *ães:*

o cidadão	the citizen	*os cidadãos*	the citizens
o alemão	the German	*os alemães*	the Germans

4. Words ending in *r* or *z* add *es:*

o mar	the sea	*os mares*	the seas
a luz	the light	*as luzes*	the lights

5. Words ending in *al, el,* and *ol,* drop the *l* and add *is:*

o animal	the animal	*os animais*	the animals
o papel	the paper	*os papéis*	the papers

---

[1] *acto, actos* ℗.

6. Words ending in stressed *il* change *l* to *s* for the plural:

civil   *civis*   civil

   Words ending in unstressed *il* change *il* to *eis* in the plural:

fácil   *fáceis*   easy

7. Words ending in *s* and stressed on the last syllable add *es* in the plural:

país   country   *países*   countries

   Words ending in *s* and not stressed on the last syllable have the same form in the plural:

o lápis   the pencil   *os lápis*   the pencils

15. THE POSSESSIVE

1. English -'s or -s' is translated by *de* "of":

o neto de Dona Maria   Dona Maria's grandson

2. Possessive adjectives and pronouns agree in number and gender with the object possessed; the adjective usually comes before the word it modifies:

meu livro   my book
meus livros   my books
minha sobrinha   my niece
minhas sobrinhas   my nieces

   Note: see Conversation Manual Lessons 14 and 15, section 32, parts 3–4.

3. In conversation *seu* tends to refer to the person spoken to and thus translates "your." However,

seu can also be used to translate "his," "her," "their." For greater clarity the prepositional form with *de* may be used:

Êles falaram de seu amigo.
They spoke of your (his, her, their) friend.

Êles falaram do amigo dêle; do amigo dela; do amigo dêles.
They spoke of his friend; of her friend; of their friend.

16. ADJECTIVES

1. Singular and plural

SINGULAR

um menino alto	a tall boy
uma menina alta	a tall girl

PLURAL

dois meninos altos	two tall boys
duas meninas altas	two tall girls

Notice that the adjective agrees with the noun it modifies in gender and number.

2. Feminine endings

a. *a* for *o* of the masculine form:

MASCULINE		FEMININE
antigo	old, ancient	*antiga*
rico	rich	*rica*
baixo	short, low	*baixa*

b. masculine form ends in *u*, feminine, in *a*:

MASCULINE		FEMININE
nu	nude, bare	*nua*
mau	bad	*má*

c. no change if masculine form ends in *e:*

MASCULINE		FEMININE
contente	happy, content	*contente*

Common exceptions:

êste[1]	this	*esta*
aquêle[2]	that	*aquela*

d. *ã* for *ão* of the masculine form:

MASCULINE .		FEMININE
alemão	German	*alemã*
cristão	Christian	*cristã*

Common exception: augmentatives (see GS23), in which *ona* replaces *ão:*

bonitão	handsome, pretty	*bonitona*

e. Adjectives ending in a consonant tend to have the same form for the masculine and the feminine:

MASCULINE		FEMININE
capaz	capable	*capaz*
comum	common	*comum*
formidável	formidable	*formidável*
simples	simple	*simples*

Examples:

Ela não é capaz de fazê-lo.
She is not able to do it.

A lição é muito simples.
The lesson is quite simple.

---

[1] *este* Ⓟ.
[2] *aquele* Ⓟ.

Common exceptions:
adjectives of nationality, *a* usually being added to the masculine form:

francês	French	*francesa*
português	Portuguese	*portuguêsa*[1]

a is added to some adjectives ending in *r*:

leitor	reader	*leitora*
diretor[2]	director	*diretora*[2]
orador	speaker, orator	*oradora*

3. *Santo* is used before names beginning with a vowel and before *Tomás* and *Gral,* and *São* is used before most other names; *Santa* is used before feminine names:

Santo Antônio[3]	Saint Anthony
o Santo Gral	the Holy Grail
São Paulo	Saint Paul
São Francisco	Saint Francis
Santa Bárbara	Saint Barbara

17. POSITION OF ADJECTIVES

1. Descriptive adjectives (which tend to distinguish persons or things from others of the same type or class) and adjectives of nationality usually come after the noun they modify:

uma casa branca	a white house

---

[1] *portuguesa* Ⓟ.
[2] *director, directora* Ⓟ.
[3] *António* Ⓟ.

uma anedota engraçada	a funny anecdote, joke
um bairro residencial	a residential district, suburb
romances contemporâneos	contemporary novels

2. Adjectives which indicate a characteristic quality of the type or class usually precede the noun:

o poderoso ditador	the powerful dictator
a verde grama	the green grass

3. Limiting adjectives, such as the demonstrative adjectives, possessive adjectives, numerals, and adjectives of quantity usually precede the noun they modify:

êste conselho	this advice
nossa conversa	our conversation
a primeira decisão	the first decision
dez dedos	ten fingers
muitas lutas	many struggles

4. Some adjectives have a different meaning according to their position; after the noun modified they have their literal (usual) meaning, and before the noun they have a figurative (extended meaning):

um homem pobre	a poor (financially) man
um pobre homem	a poor (to be pitied) man
presentes caros	expensive gifts
meu caro amigo	my dear friend
a cidade tôda[1]	all the city
tôda cidade	every city

---

[1] *toda* Ⓟ.

18. COMPARISON

1. Regular comparison

fácil	easy
mais fácil	easier
menos fácil	less easy
o mais fácil	the easier, the easiest
o menos fácil	the less easy, the least easy

2. Irregular comparison

bom	good	*melhor*	better, best
mau	bad	*pior*	worse, worst
ruim	bad	*pior*	worse, worst
muito	much	*mais*	more, most
pouco	little	*menos*	less, least
grande	big, large	*maior*	bigger, biggest
pequeno	small	*menor*	smaller, smallest
bem	well	*melhor*	better, best
mal	badly	*pior*	worse, worst

Êste livro é bom mas o outro é melhor.	This book is good but the other is better.

3. "More (less) . . . than . . ."=*mais (menos) . . . que . . .*

O português é mais fácil que o inglês.	Portuguese is easier than English.
Êle é mais inteligente do que parece.	He is more intelligent than he looks.

4. "As ... as ..." = *tão ... quanto ...*

a. before an adjective or adverb:

Tão fácil quanto...	As easy as ...
Ela fala português tão bem quanto êle.	She speaks Portuguese as well as he does.

b. before a noun the proper form of *tanto* is used:

Êste teatro não tem tantas entradas quanto aquêle.	This theatre does not have as many entrances as that one.

5. Before numerals *mais de* and *menos de* are used:

Êles têm mais de duzentas vacas.	They have more than two hundred cows.

6. An adjective may be qualified as to degree with a modifying word:

Ela está cansada.	She is tired.
Ela está muito cansada.	She is very tired.

The meaning "very" is also given by adding the proper form of *íssimo* to a word (this cannot always be done):

Ela está cansadíssima.	She is very tired.
Estamos cansadíssimos.	We are very tired.

19. PRONOUNS

Pronouns have varying forms depending on whether they are:

1. the subject of a verb
2. used after a preposition
3. the object of a verb
4. used as indirect objects
5. used with reflexive verbs
6. used to join parts of a sentence (relative pronouns)

1. Pronouns as the subject of a verb:

SINGULAR

eu	I
(tu)	(you) *(familiar)*
êle[1]	he
ela	she
o senhor	you *(masc., polite)*
a senhora	you *(fem., polite)*
você	you *(friendly)*

PLURAL

nós	we
(vós)[2]	(you)
êles[1]	they *(masc.)*
elas	they *(fem.)*
os senhores	you *(masc., polite)*
as senhoras	you *(fem., polite)*
vocês	you *(friendly)*

---

[1] *ele, eles* Ⓟ. In general, these and other variants previously cited will not be repeated.

[2] Rarely used. See Lesson 8, section 11.

SINGULAR

eu falo	I speak
(tu falas)	(you speak) *(familiar)*
êle fala	he speaks
ela fala	she speaks
o senhor fala	you speak *(masc., polite)*
a senhora fala	you speak *(fem., polite)*
você fala	you speak *(friendly)*

PLURAL

nós falamos	we speak
(vós falais)	(you speak)
êles falam	they speak *(masc.)*
elas falam	they speak *(fem.)*
os senhores falam	you speak *(masc., polite)*
as senhoras falam	you speak *(fem., polite)*
vocês falam	you speak *(friendly)*

2. Pronouns used after prepositions:

para mim	for me
(para ti)	(for you) *(familiar)*
para êle	for him
para ela	for her
para o senhor	for you *(masc., polite)*
para a senhora	for you *(fem., polite)*
para você	for you *(friendly)*
para nós	for us
(para vós)	(for you)
para êles	for them *(masc.)*
para elas	for them *(fem.)*
para os senhores	for you *(masc., polite)*
para as senhoras	for you *(fem., polite)*
para vocês	for you *(friendly)*

Notice that the form of the pronoun used after a preposition is the same as the form of the pronoun used before a verb as subject, except for *mim* "me" and *(ti)* "you" *(familiar)*.

There is a special form for "with me," *comigo* "with us," *conosco*, for "with you" *(familiar: contigo)* and for "with you, with him, with her," etc., *consigo*, although the latter form is not used frequently, *com o senhor, com êle*, etc. being preferred.

3. Pronouns used as direct objects:

me	me
(te)	(you) *(familiar)*
o	him
a	her
o	you *(masc., polite and friendly)*
a	you *(fem., polite and friendly)*
nos	us
(vos)	(you)
os	them *(masc.)*
as	them *(fem.)*
os	you *(masc., polite and friendly)*
as	you *(fem., polite and friendly)*

4. Pronouns as indirect objects:

me	to me
(te)	(to you) *(familiar)*

lhe	to him, her, you *(polite and friendly)*
nos	to us
(vos)	(to you)
lhes	to them *(masc.* and *fem.)* to you *(polite and friendly)*

Note that the subject pronouns *nós* and *vós* and the forms used after prepositions have the accent mark, that the direct and indirect object pronouns which correspond do not have the accent mark and are pronounced differently.

Inasmuch as *lhe* and *lhes* can have several meanings, a prepositional form can be used for clarity:

Eu lhe mandei uma carta.	I sent him (or her, you) a letter.
Eu mandei a ela uma carta.	I sent her a letter.

5. Reflexive pronouns:

Reflexive pronouns are used with reflexive verbs to indicate an action the subject performs upon itself:

me	myself
(te)	(yourself) *(familiar)*
se	himself, herself, yourself *(polite and friendly)*
nos	ourselves
(vos)	(yourselves)
se	themselves, yourselves *(polite and friendly)*

For more information and examples, see Lesson 15, section 32, part 10.

6. Relative pronouns:

Relative pronouns are used more in Portuguese than in English, for they are normally required, even in cases where English usage is optional (see first example below). *Que* is by far the most common form used for "that," "which," and even for "who," and "whom," although *quem* may be used for the last two. Both these forms are invariable, not changing for gender or number:

Ela disse que viria mais tarde.	She said (that) she would come later.
Êle não é o homem que (quem) me falou ontem.	He is not the man who spoke to me yesterday.

20. POSITION OF PRONOUNS

The position of object pronouns is not a fixed one, and variations will be noted in different areas. The following are given as a general guide.

1. Object pronouns usually follow the verb and are attached to the verb with a hyphen:

a. in commands:

Prometa-me isso.	Promise me that.

b. with a present participle:

oferecendo-nos mais	offering us more

    c. to avoid beginning a sentence with an object pronoun:

Abracei-o.	I embraced him.

Note: In popular speech Brazilians will at times put the pronoun before the verb in these cases.

2. Object pronouns may come before or after the verb:

    a. if the sentence begins with a pronoun or noun subject:

Êle me perdoou.	He pardoned me.
Êle perdoou-me.	He pardoned me.

    b. with infinitives:

Ela veio para me dizer a verdade.	She came to tell me the truth.
Ela veio para dizer-me a verdade.	She came to tell me the truth.

In these cases, Brazil tends to prefer the position BEFORE the verb, and Portugal AFTER the verb.

Note that if a direct object pronoun follows an infinitive the *r* of the infinitive is dropped and *l* is prefixed to the object pronoun:

Vou comprá-lo.	I am going to buy it.

3. In negative sentences and negative commands, the object pronouns precede the verb; in most other cases they tend to come before the verb:

Não o traduzimos.	We did not translate it.

Não me escreva mais.	Don't write me any more.
Êles decidiram que nos mandariam o dinheiro.	They decided that they would send us the money.
Onde o vimos?	Where did we see him?

4. If two object pronouns, one direct and the other indirect, are used as objects of the same verb the indirect comes before the direct object. This would cause the following contractions:

me + o, a, os, as = mo, ma, mos, mas
(te + o, a, os, as = to, ta, tos, tas)
lhe + o, a, os, as = lho, lha, lhos, lhas

nos + o, a, os, as = no-lo, no-la, no-los, no-las
(vos + o, a, os, as = vo-lo, vo-la, vo-los, vo-las)
lhes + o, a, os, as = lho, lha, lhos, lhas

Note: These contractions are usually avoided:

a. By using the prepositional form for the indirect object:

Eu lho dei.	I gave it to him.
Eu o dei a êle.	I gave it to him.

b. In conversation, especially in Brazil, by sometimes omitting the direct object pronoun:

Eu lhe dei.	I gave (it) to him.
Eu dei a êle.	I gave (it) to him.

5. If a direct object pronoun comes after a verb form ending in *r, s,* or *z,* this last letter is dropped and *l* is prefixed to the direct object form:

Êle fê-lo.	He did it. (The verb is *fêz*[1] from *fazer*.)
Ela vai comprá-los.	She is going to buy them. (The verb is *comprar* and the pronoun is *os*.)

Note: In conversation these combinations, except after an infinitive, are avoided:

Êle o fêz.	He did it.

If a direct object pronoun comes after a verb form which ends in a nasal sound (a vowel plus *m*), *n* is prefixed to the object pronoun:

Êles abandonaram-no.	They abandoned him.

Note: These combinations are also avoided in conversation:

a. by placing the pronoun before the verb:

Êles o abandonaram.	They abandoned him.

b. by omitting the pronoun, if the meaning is clear (reference just having been made to the object, for example):

Êles abandonaram.	They abandoned (him).

---

[1] *fez* Ⓟ.

21. SOME CONJUNCTIONS

ainda que	although
assim que	as soon as
até que	until
como	as, since
conforme	as
de maneira que	so, so that
depois que	after
e	and
embora	although
logo que	as soon as
mas	but
ou	or
para que	so that, in order that
porque	because
quando	when
se	if
segundo	as, according to

1. *e* "and"

Êle é alto e magro.	He is tall and thin.

2. *mas* "but"

Quero ir mas não posso.	I want to go but I can't.

3. *ou* "but"

Mais ou menos.	More or less.
Cinco ou seis dólares.	Five or six dollars.

4. *porque* "because"

Gosto dêle porque é muito simpático.	I like him because he is very nice.

22. QUESTION WORDS

1. *Quê?*[1] or *O quê?*[1]	"What?"
Que é que . . . ?	(with normal word order)
Que disse êle?	What did he say?
Que é que êle disse?	
2. *Por quê?*[1]	"Why?"
Por que ela não chegou antes das nove?	Why didn't she arrive before nine?
3. *Como?*	"How?"
Como se diz em português?	How do you say (it) in Portuguese?
4. *Quanto?*	"How much?"
Quanto dinheiro temos?	How much money do we have?
Quantas irmãs João tem?	How many sisters does John have?
5. *Qual? Quais?*	"Which?" "What?"
Qual é o seu?	Which one is yours?
Quais são os seus?	Which ones are yours?
6. *Quem?*	"Who?"
Quem veio com ela?	Who came with her?
7. *Onde?*	"Where?"
Onde estão os livros?	Where are the books?
8. *Quando?*	"When?"
Quando aconteceu?	When did it happen?

---

[1] When alone, or in an emphatic position, as at the end of a sentence, these forms have an accent mark.

23. ADVERBS

1. Some Portuguese adverbs are formed by adding *mente* to the feminine singular form of the adjective; this corresponds to the English ending *"ly"*:

exclusivamente   exclusively

If there are two or more adverbs with this same ending, *mente* is given only with the last one:

clara e concisamente   clearly and concisely

Adverbs are generally compared like adjectives (see GS 18).

POSITIVE	*claramente*	clearly
COMPARATIVE	*mais claramente*	more clearly
SUPERLATIVE		

2. Irregular comparatives:

bem	well	*melhor*	better, best
mal	badly	*pior*	worse, worst
muito	much	*mais*	more, most
pouco	little	*menos*	less, least

3. Adverbs and prepositions.

Many adverbs become prepositions when *de* is added:

ADVERB		PREPOSITION	
depois	afterward	*depois de*	after
antes	formerly	*antes de*	before

Other words which act similarly: *atrás* "behind";

debaixo "under"; *longe* "far"; *mais* "more"; *menos* "less"; *perto* "near."

When *que* is added to some of these they act as conjunctions:

Depois que êles	After they arrive we'll
chegarem falaremos.	talk.

4. Adverbs of time:

hoje	today
ontem	yesterday
amanhã	tomorrow
cedo	early
tarde	late
muitas vêzes[1]	often
sempre	always
nunca	never
depois	afterward
antes	before, formerly
depressa	quickly
devagar	slowly
imediatamente	immediately
raramente	seldom, rarely
agora	now

5. Adverbs of place:

aqui	here
cá	here (motion)
aí	there
ali	there (farther away)

---

[1] *vezes* Ⓟ.

lá (acolá)	there (more remote)
adiante	forward, ahead
atrás	behind
dentro	inside
fora	outside
debaixo (x = sh)	below, down
perto	near
longe	far
abaixo (x = sh)	below, under
acima	above

6. Adverbs of quantity:

muito	very, much
pouco	little
mais	more
menos	less
quanto	how much
tão	so
tanto	so much
demais, muito	too much
só, sòmente	only
apenas	only
quase	almost
bastante	enough

7. Adverbs expressing affirmation:

sim	yes
também	also
verdadeiramente	truly
certamente	truly, certainly
claro	certainly, of course
pois não!	certainly, of course

8. Advèrbs expressing negation:

não	no, not
nunca	never
já não	no longer, not now
ainda não	not yet
nem	nor
nem . . . nem	neither . . . nor

9. "Here" and "there":

Aqui "here" refers to something near the speaker.

Aí "there" refers to something near the person spoken to.

Cá "here" expresses motion toward the speaker.

Ali "there" refers to something away from the speaker and from the person spoken to.

Lá (acolá) "there" refers to something more remote.

See CM section 31, Lessons 13 and 14, for examples.

24. DIMINUTIVES AND AUGMENTATIVES

1. Certain endings, such as *inho, ote, ete,* and *ilho* imply smallness, daintiness, or even affection:

um pouco	a little
um pouquinho	a little bit
gato	cat
gatinha	kitten

sabão	soap
sabonete	a cake of toilet soap
velho	old man
velhinho	little old man
avô	grandfather
avôzinho	(dear) grandfather
avó	grandmother
avòzinha	(dear) grandmother
cedo	soon
cedinho	quite soon

2. Certain endings, such as *ão, arrão,* and *aço,* indicate large size, but they can also be uncomplimentary, indicating clumsiness, etc.:

gato	cat	*gatão, gatarrão*	big cat
homem	man	*homenzarrão*	very large man
casa	house	*casarão*	large house, mansion
drama	drama, play	*dramalhão*	melodrama
mulher	woman	*mulheraça*	big woman
mulher	woman	*mulherona*	big woman

3. NOTE: Although one should notice the difference in meaning given by these endings, he should be careful in using them and be sure he knows the form and meaning before employing words with these endings.

25. DEMONSTRATIVES

1. Demonstrative adjectives:

MASCULINE[1]	FEMININE	
êste	*esta*	this
êsse	*essa*	that
aquêle	*aquela*	that (farther removed)
êstes	*estas*	these
êsses	*essas*	those
aquêles	*aquelas*	those (farther removed)

    a. Portuguese demonstrative adjectives usually precede the nouns they modify and agree with them in gender and number:

êste menino	this boy
aquêles vizinhos	those neighbors

    b. *Êsse* and *aquêle* both mean "that." *Êsse* refers to something near to or related to the person spoken to; *aquêle* refers to something more remote:

Não gosto dêsse livro.	I don't like that book (near you or mentioned by you).
É aquêle senhor que chegou ontem.	He's that gentleman who arrived yesterday.

2. Demonstrative pronouns:

    a. The same forms are also used as demonstrative pronouns:

---

[1] These masculine forms and their contracted forms do not have an accent mark in Portugal: *este, deste,* etc.

Não quero êste sem aquêle.	I don't want this one without that one.

b. *Êste* and *aquêle* also mean "the latter" and "the former":

Acabam de chegar o embaixador (x=sh) e (o) seu secretário.	The ambassador and his secretary just arrived.
Êste é jovem e aquêle é velho.	The former is old and the latter is young.

Notice that the order in Portuguese is the opposite of the English order: *êste . . . aquêle* ("the latter . . . the former").

c. There are also some neuter forms:

isto	this, this (one)
isso	that, that (one) (near person spoken to, or mentioned by him)
aquilo	that, that (one) (farther removed)

The neuter forms are more general, referring to an idea or statement, or in referring to an object or several items thinking of them in a general way, more as "this" than "this one" or "these":

Isto é melhor que (or do que) aquilo.	This is better than that.

3. Contractions of demonstrative forms:

a. with the preposition *a*:

àquele   àqueles   àquela   àquelas   àquilo

b. with the preposition *de:*

dêste	dêstes	desta	destas	disto
dêsse	dêsses	dessa	dessas	disso
daquele	daqueles	daquela	daquelas	daquilo

c. with the preposition *em:*

neste	nestes	nesta	nestas	nisto
nesse	nesses	nessa	nessas	nisso
naquele	naqueles	naquela	naquelas	naquilo

26. INDEFINITE ADJECTIVES AND PRONOUNS

todos	all
tal (tais pl.)	such (a)
outro	another, other
alguém	somebody, someone
ninguém	nobody, no one
alguma coisa	something
nenhum	no one, none
algum	some
vários	several, some
nada	nothing
cada	each, every
tudo	all, everything
tanto	as much
certo	certain, a certain
mais	more
menos	less
qualquer	any, whatever, whoever
os demais	the rest

The adjectives above generally vary in form to agree with the word modified; *tal (tais), alguém, ninguém, nada, cada, tudo, mais,* and *menos* have only these forms.

27. NEGATION

1. *Não* "not" comes before the verb:

Não falo italiano.   I don't speak Italian.

2. There are two forms for "nothing," "never," "nobody," etc., one with and one without *não:*

Não vejo nada.	I don't see anything.
Não vou nunca.	I never go.
Não vem ninguém.	Nobody is coming.
	No one comes.

Note: this is the form used more often.

Or:

Nada vejo.	I don't see anything.
Nunca vou.	I never go.
Ninguém vem.	Nobody is coming.
	No one comes.

Also see CM section 47, lessons 22 and 23.

28. WORD ORDER

1. The usual order tends to be subject—verb—adverb—object:

João comprou lá os   John bought the Portu-
livros de português.   guese books there.

2. The tendency in Portuguese is to put the longer member of the sentence (or the emphasized part, at times) last:

João viu os seus amigos   John saw his friends in
no restaurante   the Spanish restaurant
espanhol que é na   which is on the corner.
esquina.

3. To ask a question, the same word order as for a statement can be used; this is the more common form in conversation:

João comprou lá os livros de português?	Did John buy his Portuguese books there?

A change of intonation indicates the difference between a statement and a question.

An inverted order, with the verb before the subject, can also be used, but it is much rarer:

Comprou João lá os livros de português?	Did John buy his Portuguese books there?

4. Adjectives come right after forms of the verb *ser:*

É tarde?	Is it late?
É bom?	Is it good?
A lição é fácil?	Is the lesson easy?

29. THE INFINITIVE

Portuguese uses two types of infinitives: the impersonal and the personal.

1. The impersonal infinitive is used in most cases calling for an infinitive. Practically all infinitives end in *ar* (verbs of the first conjugation): *falar* "to speak"; in *er* (second conjugation): *viver* "to live"; or in *ir* (third conjugation): *partir* "to leave."

Os alunos não querem estudar.	The students don't want to study.

2. The personal infinitive has endings which make it easier to identify the subject of the infinitive.

falar	*falarmos*
(falares)	*(falardes)*
falar	*falarem*

Thus, the personal infinitive can be used for clarity:

Parti sem me falarem.	I left without their speaking to me.
Antes de jantarmos no restaurante espanhol que está na esquina, estudamos. [1]	Before dining in the Spanish restaurant which is on the corner, we studied.

Note that the personal infinitive makes the subject of the infinitive known early in the sentence.

30. THE TENSES OF THE VERB

Portuguese verbs are generally considered under three classes or conjugations:

I—*falar*
II—*aprender*
III—*partir*

1. The present; regular verbs have the following endings added to the stem of the verb (the infinitive minus the last two letters):

I	II	III
-o	-o	-o
(-as)	(-es)	(-es)
-a	-e	-e

[1] Portugal uses an accent mark to distinguish the past tense (preterit) from the present: *estudámos, estudamos.*

-amos	*-emos*	*-imos*
(-ais)	*(-eis)*	*(-is)*
-am	*-em*	*-em*

falar to speak	*aprender* to learn	*partir* to leave
falo	*aprendo*	*parto*
(falas)	*(aprendes)*	*(partes)*
fala	*aprende*	*parte*
falamos	*aprendemos*	*partimos*
(falais)	*(aprendeis)*	*(partis)*
falam	*aprendem*	*partem*

The present can be translated in several ways:

Falo português.
{ I speak Portuguese.
I am speaking Portuguese.
I do speak Portuguese.

2. The imperfect; regular verbs have the following endings added to the stem of the verb:

I	II and III
-ava	*-ia*
(-avas)	*(-ias)*
-ava	*-ia*
-ávamos	*-íamos*
(-áveis)	*(-íeis)*
-avam	*-iam*

a. The imperfect is used:

1. to indicate continued or customary action in the past:

| *Quando eu estava em Coimbra escrevia cartas todos os dias.* | When I was in Coimbra I would write letters every day. |

2. to indicate a condition, or action in progress when something else happened:

Que lhe dizia João quando entramos?[1]	What was John telling you when we entered?

3. time of day in the past:

Eram oito horas quando voltamos.[1]	It was eight o'clock when we returned.

b. Irregular imperfects; there are four verbs in Portuguese which are irregular in the imperfect:

pôr—punha, (punhas), punha, púnhamos, (púnheis), punham
ser—era, (eras), era, éramos, (éreis), eram
ter —tinha, (tinhas), tinha, tínhamos, (tínheis), tinham
vir —vinha, (vinhas), vinha, vínhamos, (vínheis), vinham

3. The future:

The future of regular verbs is formed by adding the endings -*ei, (-ás), -á, -emos, (-eis), -ão* to the full infinitive:

falar to speak	*aprender* to learn	*partir* to leave
falarei	*aprenderei*	*partirei*
(falarás)	*(aprenderás)*	*(partirás)*
falará	*aprenderá*	*partirá*
falaremos	*aprenderemos*	*partiremos*
(falareis)	*(aprendereis)*	*(partireis)*
falarão	*aprenderão*	*partirão*

---

[1] *entrámos, voltámos* Ⓟ.

Note: The verbs *dizer, fazer,* and *trazer* add these endings to a shortened stem: *direi, farei, trarei* etc.

The future generally expresses a future action:

Chegarei às nove.   I'll arrive at nine.

Sometimes it expresses conjecture or probability in the present:

Que horas serão?   What time can it be?
Serão sete horas.   It must be seven o'clock.
Êle provàvelmente   He's probably home.
  estará em casa.

4. The preterit:

The preterit of regular verbs is formed by adding the proper endings to the stem of the verb:

I	II	III
-ei	-i	-i
(-aste)	(-este)	(-iste)
-ou	-eu	-iu
-amos (-ámos Ⓟ)	-emos	-imos
(-astes)	(-estes)	(-istes)
-aram	-eram	-iram

The preterit expresses an action completed in the past with emphasis on the fact rather than on the duration, repetition, or description:

Carlos falou comigo   Charles spoke to me
  ontem.   yesterday.
Êle me disse   He told me everything.
  (disse-me Ⓟ) tudo.
Fomos ao cinema.   We went to the movies.

Ela nos viu   She saw us.
  (viu-nos ℗).
Escrevi uma carta.   I wrote a letter.
Choveu todo o dia.   It rained all day.
Ficaram lá dois meses.   They stayed there two
                             months.

5. The present perfect:

The present perfect is formed with the present tense of *ter* (or *haver*) and the past participle of the main verb. It is used with a condition, or a continuous or repeated action, linked to the present (it is not used as much as is the present perfect in English):

Tenho (hei) aprendido   I have learned (been
  muito.   learning) very much.

6. The pluperfect:

The pluperfect is formed with the imperfect of *ter* (or *haver*) and the past participle of the main verb. It translates "had" and the past participle in English:

Quando eu cheguei,   When I arrived, he had
  êle já tinha partido.   already left.

7. The future perfect:

The future perfect is formed with the future of *ter* (or *haver*) and the past participle of the main verb:

Quando eu chegar,   When I arrive, he will
  êle já terá partido.   already have left.

Sometimes it indicates probability:

Êles já terão chegado.   They have probably
                                already arrived.

Note: Today the verb *ter* is much more commonly used than *haver* to form the perfect tenses.

31. THE SUBJUNCTIVE

The tenses given in section 30 are called tenses of the indicative. There is another set of tenses for the subjunctive. The latter indicates a certain attitude toward the statement made—uncertainty, desire, emotion, etc. Although it is used as the main verb for commands, most of the uses of the subjunctive are as a secondary verb in subordinate clauses when the statement is unreal, doubtful, indefinite, subject to some condition, or is affected by will, emotion, etc.

1. Forms

   a. The subjunctive endings of the second and third conjugations are the same.

   b. The present subjunctive is formed by adding the subjunctive endings to the stem of the first person singular, present indicative; the imperfect and future subjunctive, by removing the ending *-ram* of the third person plural of the preterit and adding the proper endings.

The subjunctive endings are as follows:

Conjugation I

PRES. SUBJ.:   *-e, -es, -e, -emos, -eis, -em*
IMPERF. SUBJ.: *-sse, -sses, -sse, -ssemos, -sseis, -ssem*
FUTURE SUBJ.: *-r, -res, -r, -rmos, -rdes, -rem*

Conjugations II and III

PRES. SUBJ.:   *-a, -as, -a, -amos, -ais, -am*
IMPERF. SUBJ.: *-sse, -sses, -sse, -'ssemos, -'sseis, -ssem*
FUTURE SUBJ.: *-r, -res, -r, -rmos, -rdes, -rem*

Note: Although the endings are different for the present subjunctive, all three conjugations have the same endings for the imperfect and future subjunctive.

EXAMPLES

	I	II	III
INFINITIVE:	*falar*	*aprender*	*partir*
PRES. SUBJ.:	*fale*	*aprenda*	*parta*
IMPERF. SUBJ.:	*falasse*	*aprendesse*	*partisse*
FUTURE SUBJ.:	*falar*	*aprender*	*partir*

2. Use of the subjunctive in commands

   a. The present subjunctive is used to express all polite commands and negative familiar commands:

Abra a janela, por favor.	Open the window, please.
Não abra a janela.	Don't open the window.
Não abras a janela.	Don't open the window (fam.).

   b. To indicate a desire or wish, and in indirect commands, with or without *que:*

(Que) viva o presidente!	Long live the President!
Que venham cedo.	Have them come early.
Não digamos mais.	Let's not say any more.

3. Other uses of the subjunctive

  a. The subjunctive is used after verbs of desire, request, permission, approval, disapproval, and the like:

Quero que êle venha cedo.	I want him to come early.
Eu gostaria (de) que êle viesse cedo.	I should like for him to come early.

  b. after verbs of emotion (to be happy, to be sorry, and the like):

Estamos contentes (de) que ela chegasse cedo.	We are glad that she arrived early.
Sinto muito que êles não possam vir.	I am very sorry that they cannot come.

  c. after verbs of doubt or denial:

Duvido (de) que êle venha hoje.	I doubt he will come today.
Não acho que seja verdade.	I don't believe it is true.
Não estamos certos (de) que ela venha.	We are not sure she will come.

Note: If the subject of the two verbs is the same, the infinitive tends to be used, instead of the subjunctive, for the second verb:

Quero chegar cedo.	I want to arrive early.
Sinto muito não poder ir.	I am very sorry I can't go.
Duvido poder ir hoje.	I doubt I can go today.

  d. after impersonal verbs ("it is possible," etc.) which do not express certainty:

É possível que êle o faça. It is possible that he will
do it.
É preciso que cheguemos It is necessary that we
antes das nove. arrive before nine.

Note: If the statement is general and there is no
specific subject for the second verb the infinitive
is used:

É possível fazê-lo. It is possible to do it.
É preciso chegar antes It is necessary to arrive
das nove. before nine.

e. The subjunctive is used after various conjunctive adverbs.

1. Certain conjunctive adverbs tend to be
followed regularly by the subjunctive:

Êle me escreveu para He wrote me in order
que (or *afim de que*) that I know the news.
eu soubesse a notícia.

2. Some conjunctions, as *de forma que, de
maneira que, de modo que,* "so," "so that,"
are followed by the subjunctive if they indicate a purpose not yet attained, and by the
indicative if they indicate a result in the past:

Corri de maneira que I ran so that I would
chegasse na hora. arrive on time.
Não corri, de maneira I didn't run, so I didn't
que não cheguei na arrive on time.
hora.

Ainda que and *embora* "although" tend to follow
this pattern in Portugal, although in Brazil they
are usually followed by the subjunctive in all
cases:

Embora estudasse, não aprendi muito.	Although I studied, I didn't learn much.

3. Certain conjunctions are followed by the subjunctive if the verb indicates a condition or action in the future; otherwise by the indicative. Among the conjunctions which are followed by the present or future subjunctive are *até que* "until," *como* "as," *conforme* "as, according as," *quando* "when," *segundo* "as, according as":

Eu lhes falo quando chegarem (fut. subj.).	I'll speak to them when they arrive.
Eu lhes falei quando chegaram (preterit, past tense).	I spoke to them when they arrived.

4. The subjunctive is used after a relative pronoun with a negative or indefinite antecedent and in some indefinite or alternate types of expressions:

Quero um livro que me explique isto.	I want a book that will explain this to me.
Não há ninguém aqui que fale russo.	There is nobody here who speaks Russian.
Seja como fôr[1] . . .	Be that as it may . . .
Como Deus quiser.	As God wishes.

5. The future subjunctive can be used as indicated in section 4; it is especially used after conjunctions of time, such as *ao passo que* "while," *assim que* "as soon as," *depois que* "after," *enquanto* "while," *logo que* "as soon

---

[1] *for* Ⓟ.

as," *quando* "when," and a few others, when it is expressing future time; when the first verb is in the past, the imperfect subjunctive is used; if the verb after the conjunction expresses past time the indicative is used:

Vamos decidir assim que nos disserem (fut. subj.).	We'll decide as soon as they tell us.
Indicamos[1] que decidiríamos assim que nos dissessem (imperfect subj.).	We said that we would decide as soon as they told us.
Assim que nos disseram, decidimos (preterit).	As soon as they told us, we decided.
Eu lhe mando o livro depois que êle me mandar (fut. subj.) *o dinheiro.*	I'll send him the book after he sends me the money.
Êle me dirá quando me vir.	He will tell me when he sees me. (*Vir* is the future subjunctive of *ver.*)

6. The subjunctive is used in certain conditional sentences (see section 34).

32. SEQUENCE OF TENSES

In addition to information already given, keep in mind the following regarding sequence of tenses:

1. If the main verb is in the present or future,

---

[1] *indicámos* Ⓟ.

the subjunctive, if required, will be in the present if its time is present or future:

Duvido (de) que êle venha.	I doubt that he will come.
Duvido (de) que elas estejam em casa.	I doubt that they are home.

The subjunctive will be in the imperfect if its time is past:

Duvido que êle viesse.	I doubt that he came.

2. If the main verb is in the past, the subjunctive, if required, will be in the imperfect if it reflects action at the same time or later; it will be in the pluperfect (past perfect subjunctive) if it indicates previous action:

Eu duvidava (de) que êle viesse.	I doubted that he would come.
Eu duvidava (de) que êle tivesse vindo.	I doubted that he had come.

33. THE CONDITIONAL

1. The present conditional is formed by adding the endings *–ia, –ias, –ia, –íamos –íeis, –iam* to the infinitives of all three conjugations:

I	II	III
falar to speak	*aprender* to learn	*partir* to leave
falaria	*aprenderia*	*partiria*
(falarias)	*(aprenderias)*	*(partirias)*
falaria	*aprenderia*	*partiria*

falaríamos	*aprenderíamos*	*partiríamos*
(falaríeis)	*(aprenderíeis)*	*(partiríeis)*
falariam	*aprenderiam*	*partiriam*

Note: The verbs *dizer, fazer,* and *trazer* add these endings to a shortened stem: *diria, faria, traria,* etc.

2. The conditional is used to express:

   a. a future from a past point, being usually translated "would" and the meaning of the verb:

Êle me disse que chegaria às sete.	He told me that he would arrive at seven.

   b. probability or conjecture in the past:

Seriam oito horas, quando êle chegou.	It was probably eight o'clock when he arrived.
Que horas seriam quando êle chegou?	What time could it have been (I wonder what time it was) when he arrived?

   c. a softened statement:

Eu gostaria de vê-lo.	I would (should) like to see him.

   d. the conclusion of certain conditional sentences (see section 34, following)

3. The perfect conditional is formed with the conditional of *ter* (*haver* is used sometimes) and the past participle of the main verb:

| *Êle me teria falado . . .* | He would have spoken to me . . . |
| *Elas não teriam ido . . .* | They would not have gone . . . |

34. CONDITIONAL SENTENCES

Conditional sentences have two parts, the conditional or "if" clause and the conclusion. The following are the most common combinations.

1. A simple condition can be expressed with both verbs in the indicative. Sometimes the "if" factor is the equivalent of "when" or "whenever":

Se chove (está chovendo), não vamos.	If it is raining, we won't go.
Se êle entrou eu não o vi.	If he came in, I didn't see him.
Se êle chegava cedo vinha me ver.	If (whenever) he arrived early, he came to see me.

2. When the "if" clause expresses a simple condition (not a doubtful one) in the future, the future subjunctive (or the present indicative at times) is used in the "if" clause and the future indicative (or the present indicative) is used in the conclusion:

| *Se chover (chove) não iremos (vamos).* | If it rains we won't go. |

3. When the "if" clause expresses a doubtful condition in the future the imperfect subjunctive is
used in the "if" clause and the conditional (or
the imperfect indicative)[1] in the conclusion:

Se chovesse não iríamos (íamos).	If it should rain we would not go.

The same sequence is used to indicate a doubtful
or contrary-to-fact situation in the present:

Se eu fôsse[2] rico viajaria (viajava) todos os verões.	If I were rich I would travel every summer.

4. When the "if" clause expresses a condition contrary-to-fact in the past the pluperfect (past perfect) subjunctive is used in the "if" clause and
the conditional perfect (or the pluperfect indicative)[3] in the conclusion:

Se tivesse chovido não teríamos (tínhamos) ido.	If it had rained we would not have gone.

35. COMMANDS AND REQUESTS

There are two types of commands, familiar commands and polite, or less familiar, commands.

1. Familiar commands

Familiar commands are used with people with

---

[1] The imperfect indicative is usually preferred in conversation.

[2] *fosse* Ⓟ.

[3] Preferred in conversation.

whom one would use *tu* and its verb forms (see section 11 of Lesson 8). The familiar imperative forms in the singular usually correspond to the third person singular of the present indicative and to the second person plural *(familiar)* without the final *s:*

INFINITIVE	SINGULAR	PLURAL	
falar	*(fala)*	*(falai)*	speak
aprender	*(aprende)*	*(aprendei)*	learn
partir	*(parte)*	*(parti)*	leave

These forms are used to give only affirmative familiar commands. For negative familiar commands the second and fifth forms (both *familiar*) of the present subjunctive are used:

INFINITIVE	SINGULAR	PLURAL	
falar	*não fales*	*não faleis*	don't speak
aprender	*não aprendas*	*não aprendais*	don't learn
partir	*não partas*	*não partais*	don't leave

Note: As explained before, these forms are generally to be avoided until the student understands their use and has occasion to use them.

2. Polite commands

Practically all commands, affirmative or negative, will be given with the third singular and plural forms of the present subjunctive. These forms will usually correspond to the third singular and plural forms of the present indicative but with final *a* changed to *e* and final *e* changed to *a* (but also see grammar summary section 31, part 1 b):

INDICATIVE	SUBJUNCTIVE
Êle fala. He speaks.	*Fale!* Speak!
	Não fale! Don't speak!
Êles falam. They speak.	*Falem.* Speak.
	Não falem! Don't speak!
Êle aprende. He learns.	*Aprenda!* Learn!
	Não aprenda! Don't learn!
Êles aprendem. They learn	*Aprendam!* Learn!
	Não aprendam! Don't learn!
Êle parte. He leaves	*Parta!* Leave!
	Não parta! Don't leave!
Êles partem. They leave.	*Partam!* Leave!
	Não partam! Don't leave.

Other Examples:

Escreva-o.	Write it.
Venha amanhã.	Come tomorrow.
Diga-me a verdade.	Tell me the truth.
Escute!	Listen!
Termine tudo antes das cinco, por favor.	Finish everything before five, please.

Negative Examples:

Não me escreva mais!	Don't write me any more!
Não venha antes das oito.	Don't come before eight.
Não dancem mais.	Don't dance any more.
Não gastem todo o dinheiro.	Don't spend all the money.

Note that object pronouns follow affirmative commands and are attached to the verb with a hyphen (in Brazilian speech pronouns may precede the verb sometimes). In negative commands the object pronouns precede the verb.

3. Indirect commands

Indirect commands are also given with the subjunctive (*que* may precede the verb):

Que entrem!	Let (have) them come in.
(Que) venham amanhã.	Let them come tomorrow.
Que não volte mais.	Let him never return.
Viva o Brasil!	Long live Brazil!
Viva Portugal!	Long live Portugal!
Deus nos guarde!	May God protect us!

4. Commands with reflexive verbs

Reflexive pronouns follow the order indicated in part 2 immediately above:

SINGULAR

Sente-se.	Sit down.
Deite-se cedo.	Go to bed early.
Vista-se.	Dress.
Não se esqueça.	Don't forget.

PLURAL

Sentem-se.	Sit down.
Deitem-se cedo.	Go to bed early.
Vistam-se.	Dress.
Não se esqueçam.	Don't forget.

36. THE PARTICIPLE

1. The present participle is formed by adding *-ando,
-endo,* and *-indo* to the stems of verbs of the three
conjugations:

I		II	
falar	to speak	*aprender*	to learn
falando	speaking	*aprendendo*	learning

III	
partir	to leave
partindo	leaving

If an object pronoun follows the present participle it is joined to it with a hyphen:

falando-nos	speaking to us
escrevendo-lhe	writing to him
vendo-o	seeing him

2. The present participle is used in the progressive
tenses (see section 37 which follows) and often
much as in English:

Vi-o na praia, dormindo.	I saw him on the beach, sleeping.
Partindo (Ao partir), êle me deu seu cartão.	On leaving he gave me his card.

3. The past participle is formed by adding *-ado,
-ido, -ido* to the stems of verbs of the three conjugations:

I		II	
falar	to speak	*aprender*	to learn
falado	spoken	*aprendido*	learned

III

partir	to leave
partido	left

4. Irregular participles

Pôr has the irregular present participle *pondo*.

The following are some of the verbs which have irregular past participles:

INFINITIVE		IRREGULAR PAST PARTICIPLE
abrir	to open	*aberto*
cobrir	to cover	*coberto*
dizer	to say	*dito*
escrever	to write	*escrito*
fazer	to do, make	*feito*
pôr	to put	*pôsto (posto ℗)*
ver	to see	*visto*
vir	to come	*vindo*

Some verbs have a regular participle and also a shortened form:

INFINITIVE		REGULAR	IRREGULAR
aceitar	to accept	*aceitado*	*aceito, aceite*
entregar	to deliver, give	*entregado*	*entregue*
ganhar	to earn, gain	*ganhado*	*ganho*
gastar	to spend	*gastado*	*gasto*
pagar	to pay	*pagado*	*pago*
morrer	to die	*morrido*	*morto*

* rarely used today

Although both forms are used, there is a tendency for the regular form to be favored as the past participle of the perfect tenses and for the shortened form to be favored as an adjective:

Tínhamos aceitado todo o dinheiro.	We had accepted all the money.
O dinheiro não foi aceito.	The money was not accepted.

37. PROGRESSIVE TENSES

The Portuguese progressive tenses are formed with the present participle and the tenses of *estar* (although other verbs, such as *ir* may also be used as the auxiliary verb):

Estou estudando.	I am studying.
Quando êles entraram na sala nós estávamos lendo o jornal.	When they entered the room we were reading the newspaper.
Elas estão divertindo-se.	They are having a good time.
Êles iam cantando.	They were singing. ("They went on singing.")

Portugal also uses *estar a* and the infinitive: *Estou a estudar.* I am studying.

38. THE PASSIVE VOICE

The passive voice is made up of the forms of *ser* with the past participle:

O Brasil foi descoberto em 1500 (mil e quinhentos).	Brazil was discovered in 1500.

The passive voice is used as in English. Very often, however, Portuguese uses *se* to express the passive (see part 10 of Lesson 15).

39. TO BE

Ser and *estar* both mean "to be" in Portuguese. In general *ser* indicates a characteristic or permanent state and *estar* a temporary one. However, one should note the different uses of these verbs.

SER	ESTAR	
eu sou	*eu estou*	I am
(tu és)	*(tu estás)*	you are *(familiar)*
o senhor é	*o senhor está*	you are *(masc.)*
a senhora é	*a senhora está*	you are *(fem.)*
você é	*você está*	you are
êle é	*êle está*	he is
ela é	*ela está*	she is
nós somos	*nós estamos*	we are
(vós sois)	*(vós estais)*	(you are)
os senhores são	*os senhores estão*	you are
as senhoras são	*as senhoras estão*	you are
vocês são	*vocês estão*	you are
êles são	*êles estão*	they are
elas são	*elas estão*	they are

SER

1. indicates a characteristic or inherent quality:

Meu irmão é alto.	My brother is tall.
O livro é vermelho.	The book is red.
Ela é jovem.	She is young.
O gêlo[1] é frio.	Ice is cold.
Êle é inteligente.	He is intelligent.

2. indicates an established or permanent location:

A capital é no Distrito Federal.	The capital is in the Federal District.
A escola é longe daqui.	The school is far from here.

3. is used with a predicate noun or pronoun:

Êle é professor.	He is a professor.
Ela é aluna.	She is a student.
Somos americanos.	We are Americans.
É êle.	It is he.
Sou eu.	It is I.

4. indicates origin or source:

Êle é de Lisboa.	He's from Lisbon.
Esta madeira é do Brasil.	This wood is from Brazil.

5. indicates material:

A casa é de pedra.	The house is made of stone.

---

[1] *gelo* Ⓟ.

6. indicates possession:

Os livros são dêle.	The books are his.
De quem é?	Whose is it?
É meu.	It is mine.

7. is used in indicating the time:

São duas horas.	It is two o'clock.
É meio-dia.	It is noon.

8. is used in impersonal expressions:

É tarde.	It is late.
É cedo.	It is early.
É possível.	It is possible.
É pena.	It's a pity.
Não é verdade?	Isn't it so?

9. is used in forming the passive voice (see section
   38 above)

ESTAR

1. expresses temporary position or location:

Êle não está aqui.	He is not here.
Maria está em casa.	Mary is home.
Onde estão os livros?	Where are the books?
O jornal está na caixa *(x = sh).*	The newspaper is in the box.

2. indicates a temporary quality or characteristic:

Ela está contente.	She is happy (pleased).
Estamos cansados.	We are tired.
Estou pronto.	I'm ready.

O café está frio.	The coffee is cold.
A janela está aberta (fechada).	The window is open (closed).
Ela está bonita hoje.	She is pretty today.

3. is used to form the progressive tenses (see section 37 above):

Êles estão falando (a falar) de nós.	They are talking about us.

4. is used in expressions about the weather:

Está frio hoje.	It is cold today.
No verão estará quente.	It will be hot in the summer.

5. is used in certain other expressions (especially in Brazil):

Estou com fome.	I am hungry.
Êles estão com sêde.[1]	They are thirsty.

Note: The verb *ficar* "to remain" is quite popular in Brazil and is often used for *ser* or *estar*:

Onde fica a estação?	Where is the station?
Fica longe daqui.	It is far from here.
Ela fica contente.	She is happy (pleased).
Êle ficou doente.	He became ill.

---

[1] *sede* Ⓟ.

40. THE FORMS OF THE REGULAR VERB

CONJUGATION I   CONJUGATION II   CONJUGATION III

INFINITIVE

PRESENT

falar to speak   *aprender* to learn   *partir* to leave

PERSONAL INFINITIVE

falar	*aprender*	*partir*
(falares)	*(aprenderes)*	*(partires)*
falar	*aprender*	*partir*
falarmos	*aprendermos*	*partirmos*
(falardes)	*(aprenderdes)*	*(partirdes)*
falarem	*aprenderem*	*partirem*

PAST

ter falado	*ter aprendido*	*ter partido*
to have spoken	to have learned	to have left

PARTICIPLES

PRESENT

falando	*aprendendo*	*partindo*
speaking	learning	leaving

PAST

falado spoken   *aprendido* learned   *partido* left

INDICATIVE AND CONDITIONAL

PRESENT

falo   *aprendo*   *parto*

(falas)	*(aprendes)*	*(partes)*
fala	*aprende*	*parte*
falamos	*aprendemos*	*partimos*
(falais)	*(aprendeis)*	*(partis)*
falam	*aprendem*	*partem*

IMPERFECT

falava	*aprendia*	*partia*
(falavas)	*(aprendias)*	*(partias)*
falava	*aprendia*	*partia*
falávamos	*aprendíamos*	*partíamos*
(faláveis)	*(aprendíeis)*	*(partíeis)*
falavam	*aprendiam*	*partiam*

PRETERIT

falei	*aprendi*	*parti*
(falaste)	*(aprendeste)*	*(partiste)*
falou	*aprendeu*	*partiu*
falamos[1]	*aprendemos*	*partimos*
(falastes)	*(aprendestes)*	*(partistes)*
falaram	*aprenderam*	*partiram*

FUTURE

falarei	*aprenderei*	*partirei*
(falarás)	*(aprenderás)*	*(partirás)*
falará	*aprenderá*	*partirá*
falaremos	*aprenderemos*	*partiremos*
(falareis)	*(aprendereis)*	*(partireis)*
falarão	*aprenderão*	*partirão*

---

[1] *falámos* Ⓟ.

CONDITIONAL

falaria	*aprenderia*	*partiria*
(falarias)	*(aprenderias)*	*(partirias)*
falaria	*aprenderia*	*partiria*
falaríamos	*aprenderíamos*	*partiríamos*
(falaríeis)	*(aprenderíeis)*	*(partiríeis)*
falariam	*aprenderiam*	*partiriam*

PRESENT PERFECT

tenho	*falado*	*aprendido*	*partido*
(tens)	*falado*	*aprendido*	*partido*
tem	*falado*	*aprendido*	*partido*
temos	*falado*	*aprendido*	*partido*
(tendes)	*falado*	*aprendido*	*partido*
têm	*falado*	*aprendido*	*partido*

PLUPERFECT (COMPOUND)

tinha	*falado*	*aprendido*	*partido*
(tinhas)	*falado*	*aprendido*	*partido*
tinha	*falado*	*aprendido*	*partido*
tínhamos	*falado*	*aprendido*	*partido*
(tínheis)	*falado*	*aprendido*	*partido*
tinham	*falado*	*aprendido*	*partido*

PLUPERFECT (SIMPLE)[1]

falara	*aprendera*	*partira*
(falaras)	*(aprenderas)*	*(partiras)*
falara	*aprendera*	*partira*

---

[1] The simple pluperfect has the same meaning as the compound pluperfect, but it is more a literary tense and is not ordinarily used in conversation.

faláramos	aprendêramos	partíramos
(faláreis)	(aprendêreis)	(partíreis)
falara	aprendera	partira

FUTURE PERFECT

terei	falado	aprendido	partido
(terás)	falado	aprendido	partido
terá	falado	aprendido	partido
teremos	falado	aprendido	partido
(tereis)	falado	aprendido	partido
terão	falado	aprendido	partido

CONDITIONAL PERFECT

teria	falado	aprendido	partido
(terias)	falado	aprendido	partido
teria	falado	aprendido	partido
teríamos	falado	aprendido	partido
(teríeis)	falado	aprendido	partido
teriam	falado	aprendido	partido

SUBJUNCTIVE

PRESENT

fale	aprenda	parta
(fales)	(aprendas)	(partas)
fale	aprenda	parta
falemos	aprendamos	partamos
(faleis)	(aprendais)	(partais)
falem	aprendam	partam

IMPERFECT

falasse	*aprendesse*	*partisse*
(falasses)	*(aprendesses)*	*(partisses)*
falasse	*aprendesse*	*partisse*
falássemos	*aprendêssemos*	*partíssemos*
(falásseis)	*(aprendêsseis)*	*(partísseis)*
falassem	*aprendessem*	*partissem*

FUTURE

falar	*aprender*	*partir*
(falares)	*(aprenderes)*	*(partires)*
falar	*aprender*	*partir*
falarmos	*aprendermos*	*partirmos*
(falardes)	*(aprenderdes)*	*(partirdes)*
falarem	*aprenderem*	*partirem*

PRESENT PERFECT

tenha	*falado*	*aprendido*	*partido*
(tenhas)	*falado*	*aprendido*	*partido*
tenha	*falado*	*aprendido*	*partido*
tenhamos	*falado*	*aprendido*	*partido*
(tenhais)	*falado*	*aprendido*	*partido*
tenham	*falado*	*aprendido*	*partido*

PLUPERFECT

tivesse	*falado*	*aprendido*	*partido*
(tivesses)	*falado*	*aprendido*	*partido*
tivesse	*falado*	*aprendido*	*partido*
tivéssemos	*falado*	*aprendido*	*partido*
(tivésseis)	*falado*	*aprendido*	*partido*
tivessem	*falado*	*aprendido*	*partido*

IMPERATIVE

I
Familiar

(Fala) (tu)!	Speak *(sing.)!*
(Falai) (vós!)	Speak *(pl.)!*
(Não fales) (tu)!	Don't speak *(sing.)!*
(Não faleis) (vós)!	Don't speak *(pl.)!*

Polite

Fale (o senhor, você)!	Speak *(sing.)!*
Falem (os senhores, vocês)!	Speak *(pl.)!*
Não fale (o senhor, você)!	Don't speak *(sing.)!*
Não falem (os senhores, vocês)!	Don't speak *(pl.)!*
Falemos (nós)!	*Let's speak!*

II
Familiar

(Aprende) (tu)!	Learn *(sing.)!*
(Aprendei) (vós)!	Learn *(pl.)!*
(Não aprendas) (tu)!	Don't learn *(sing.)!*
(Não aprendais) (vós)!	Don't learn *(pl.)!*

Polite

Aprenda (o senhor, você)!	Learn *(sing.)!*
Aprendam (os senhores, vocês)!	Learn *(pl.)!*
Não aprenda (o senhor, você)!	Don't learn *(sing.)!*

Não aprendam (os senhores, vocês)!	Don't learn *(pl.)!*
Aprendamos (nós)!	Let's learn!

III

Familiar

(Parte) (tu)!	Leave *(sing.)!*
(Parti) (vós)!	Leave *(pl.)!*
(Não partas) (tu)!	Don't leave *(sing.)!*
(Não partais) (vós)!	Don't leave *(pl.)!*

Polite

Parta *(o senhor, você)!*	Leave *(sing.)!*
Partam *(os senhores, vocês)!*	Leave *(pl.)!*
Não parta (o senhor, você)!	Don't leave *(sing.)!*
Não partam (os senhores, vocês)!	Don't leave *(pl.)!*
Partamos (nós)!	Let's leave!

41. RADICAL-CHANGING VERBS

As indicated before (see Lesson 1, Vowels) the sound of vowels varies in Portuguese, with open and closed qualities for the same vowel, as well as other variations. To have good pronunciation it is necessary to distinguish between these sounds. Certain verbs in Portuguese have variations in the stem (or radical, as it is also called) and these should be kept in mind. *Only some of these changes, with a few sample verbs, are given here.* Unless otherwise indi-

cated, the change given will pertain to those forms
of the verb in which the stress falls on the last vowel
of the stem: the 1, 2, 3, and 6 forms (the three singular and the third plural forms) of the present indicative and of the present subjunctive.

I

levar	to take away	} open *e*
secar	to dry	

cortar	to cut	
escovar	to brush	
jogar	to play (game)	} open *o*
morar	to dwell, live	
notar	to note	
voltar	to return	

cear	to eat supper	
estrear	to use, wear for the first time	*e* changes to *ei*
passear	to take a walk or ride	
recear	to fear	

odiar	to hate	} *i* chances to *ei*
remediar	to remedy	

II

dever	to owe, to have to	*e* changes to open *e* in 2, 3, 6 (not in 1st form)
escrever	to write	
meter	to put	

correr	to run	} open *o* in 2, 3, 6
mover	to move	

III

competir	to compete	
conferir	to confer	
conseguir	to obtain	
despir (–se)	to undress (oneself)	*e* becomes *i* in 1;
divertir (*–se*)	to amuse (oneself)	*e* becomes open *e* in 2, 3, 6 of pres. ind.;
ferir	to wound	
preferir	to prefer	*e* becomes *i* in all 6 forms of pres. subj.
referir	to refer	
repetir	to repeat	
seguir	to follow	
servir	to serve	
vestir (*–se*)	to dress (oneself)	

mentir	to lie	*e* becomes *i* in 1 of pres. ind. and in all pres. subj.
sentir	to feel, to be sorry	

cobrir	to cover	*o* becomes *u* in 1; *o* becomes open *o* in 2, 3, 6 of pres. ind.; *o* becomes *u* in all 6 forms of pres. subj.
dormir	to sleep	
engolir	to swallow	
tossir	to cough	

consumir	to consume	*u* becomes open *o* in 2, 3, 6 of pres. ind.
fugir	to flee	
sacudir	to shake	
subir	to go up	

42. SPELLING CHANGES IN VERBS

Some verb forms, as is true of other parts of speech, undergo spelling changes before certain endings. These changes are in the final consonant of the stem. To understand these cases better, consult section 2, on pronunciation, of this grammar summary.

1. Verbs ending in *-car*

In verbs ending in *-car* in the infinitive the *c* changes to *qu* before *e*. This occurs in:
a. the first person singular of the preterit
b. all forms of the present subjunctive

Example: *ficar* to remain, to be

PRETERIT INDICATIVE	PRESENT SUBJUNCTIVE
fiquei	*fique*
(ficaste)	*(fiques)*
ficou	*fique*
ficamos[1]	*fiquemos*
(ficastes)	*(fiqueis)*
ficaram	*fiquem*

Some of the other verbs in *-car:*

atacar	to attack	*secar*	to dry
educar	to educate	*significar*	to signify, mean
explicar	to explain		
indicar	to indicate	*tocar*	to touch, play (music)
		verificar	to verify

---

[1] *ficámos* Ⓟ.

2. Verbs ending in *-çar*

In these verbs the *ç* changes to *c* before *e*, that is, in the same forms indicated above.

Example: *começar* to begin

PRETERIT INDICATIVE	PRESENT SUBJUNCTIVE
comecei	*comece*
(começaste)	*(comeces)*
começou	*comece*
começamos[1]	*comecemos*
(começastes)	*(comeceis)*
começaram	*comecem*

Some of the other verbs in *-çar:*

abraçar	to embrace	*forçar*	to force
alcançar	to reach	*recomeçar*	to begin again
caçar	to hunt		
		traçar	to trace, sketch

3. Verbs ending in *-gar*

In these verbs *g* becomes *gu* before *e*, that is, in the same forms indicated above.

Example: *chegar* to arrive

PRETERIT INDICATIVE	PRESENT SUBJUNCTIVE
cheguei	*chegue*
(chegaste)	*(chegues)*
chegou	*chegue*
chegamos[2]	*cheguemos*
(chegastes)	*(chegueis)*
chegaram	*cheguem*

---

[1] *começámos* Ⓟ.
[2] *chegámos* Ⓟ.

Some of the other verbs in *-gar:*

apagar	to put out, erase	*jogar*	to play (game)
carregar	to load, transport	*pegar*	to seize
		pagar	to pay
entregar	to deliver	*rogar*	to beg, ask
fatigar	to fatigue		

4. Verbs ending in *-cer*

In these verbs *c* changes to *ç* before *o* or *a*. This occurs in:
   a. the first person singular of the present indicative
   b. all forms of the present subjunctive

Example: *conhecer* to know

PRESENT INDICATIVE	PRESENT SUBJUNCTIVE
conheço	*conheça*
(conheces)	*(conheças)*
conhece	*conheça*
conhecemos	*conheçamos*
(conheceis)	*(conheçais)*
conhecem	*conheçam*

Some of the other verbs in *-cer:*

abastecer	to supply	*favorecer*	to favor
acontecer	to happen	*fornecer*	to supply
agradecer	to be grateful	*merecer*	to deserve
aparecer	to appear	*nascer*	to be born
carecer	to lack		
compadecer	to pity	*obedecer*	to obey

desaparecer	to disappear	oferecer	to offer
desobedecer	to disobey	padecer	to suffer
envelhecer	to age	parecer	to seem
esquecer	to forget	permanecer	to remain
falecer	to die	pertencer	to belong
		reconhecer	to recognize

5. Verbs ending in -ger

In these verbs g changes to j before o or a, that is, in the same forms indicated above.

Example: proteger to protect

PRESENT INDICATIVE

protejo
(proteges)
protege

protegemos
(protegeis)
protegem

PRESENT SUBJUNCTIVE

proteja
(protejas)
proteja

protejamos
(protejais)
protejam

Some of the other verbs in -ger:

eleger	to elect	reger	to rule

6. Verbs ending in -gir

These verbs have the same changes as verbs ending in -ger. Some of these are:

dirigir	to direct	fugir	to flee
erigir	to erect	surgir	to emerge
exigir (x = sh)	to demand		

7. Verbs ending in *-guer* or *-guir*

In these verbs *gu* changes to *g* before *o* or *a*. This occurs in the same forms as in section 4 above.

Example: *distinguir* to distinguish

PRESENT INDICATIVE	PRESENT SUBJUNCTIVE
distingo	*distinga*
(distingues)	*(distingas)*
distingue	*distinga*
distinguimos	*distingamos*
(distinguis)	*(distingais)*
distinguem	*distingam*

Some verbs in *-guer* and *-guir:*

erguer	to raise	*extinguir*	to extinguish
		perseguir	to pursue
conseguir	to obtain	*seguir*	to follow

Seguir is also radical changing (see section 41 above, part III) and it and its derivatives (such as *conseguir* and *perseguir*) will show these changes:

PRESENT INDICATIVE	PRESENT SUBJUNCTIVE
sigo	*siga*
(segues)	*(sigas)*
segue	*siga*
seguimos	*sigamos*
(seguis)	*(sigais)*
seguem	*sigam*

43. IRREGULAR VERBS

Some of the irregular verbs in Portuguese will be given below. Only tenses which have irregular forms will be given. Verbs with only radical changes or orthographic changes will not be given. Imperative forms will not be listed. Irregular participles will be indicated.

Abrir to open

1. PAST PART.: *aberto*

Caber to fit in

1. PRES. IND.: *caibo, cabes, cabe, cabemos, cabeis, cabem*

2. PRES. SUBJ.: *caiba, caibas, caiba, caibamos, caibais, caibam*

3. PRET. IND.: *coube, coubeste, coube, coubemos, coubestes, couberam*

4. PLUP. IND.: *coubera, couberas, coubera, coubéramos, coubéreis, couberam*

5. IMPF. SUBJ.: *coubesse, coubesses, coubesse, coubéssemos, coubésseis, coubessem*

6. FUT. SUBJ.: *couber, couberes, couber, coubermos, couberdes, couberem*

Cair to fall

Like *sair* to leave. See below.

Cobrir to cover

1. PAST. PART.: *coberto*

Conduzir to conduct, lead (to)

1. PRES. IND.: *conduzo, conduzes, conduz, conduzimos, conduzis, conduzem*

Construir to construct

1. PRES. IND.: *construo, construis, construi,
construímos, construís, construem*

also

PRES. IND.: *construo, constróis, constrói,
construímos, construís, constroem*

2. IMPF. IND.: *construía, construías, construía,
construíamos, construíeis, construíam*

3. PRET. IND.: *construí, construíste, construiu,
construímos, construístes, construíram*

5. PLUP. IND.: *construíra, construíras, construíra,
construíramos, construíreis,
construíram*

6. IMPF. SUBJ.: *construísse, construísses, construísse,
construíssemos, construísseis,
construíssem*

7. FUT. SUBJ.: *construir, construíres, construir,
construirmos, construirdes,
construírem*

8. PAST PART.: *construído*

Crer to believe

1. PRES. IND.: *creio, crês, crê, cremos, credes, crêem*

2. PRES. SUBJ.: *creia, creias, creia, creiamos, creiais,
creiam*

3. PRET. IND.: *cri, crêste,[1] creu, cremos, crêstes,[1]
creram*

Dar to give

1. PRES. IND.: *dou, dás, dá, damos, dais, dão*

---

[1] No accent mark in Portugal.

2. PRES. SUBJ.:   *dê, dês, dê, demos,*[1] *deis, dêem*

3. PRET. IND.:   *dei, deste, deu, demos, destes, deram*

4. PLUP. IND.:   *dera, deras, dera, déramos, déreis,*
deram

5. IMPF. SUBJ.:   *desse, desses, desse, déssemos, désseis,*
dessem

6. FUT. SUBJ.:   *der, deres, der, dermos, derdes, derem*

Despedir to send away

1. PRES. IND.:   *despeço, despedes, despede,*
despedimos, despedis, despedem

2. PRES. SUBJ.:   *despeça, despeças, despeça,*
despeçamos, despeçais, despeçam

Dizer to say

1. PRES. IND.:   *digo, dizes, diz, dizemos, dizeis, dizem*

2. PRES. SUBJ.:   *diga, digas, diga, digamos, digais,*
digam

3. PRET. IND.:   *disse, dissesste, disse, dissemos,*
dissesstes, disseram

4. PLUP. IND.:   *dissera, disseras, dissera, disséramos,*
disséreis, disseram

5. IMP. SUBJ.:   *dissesse, dissesses, dissesse,*
disséssemos, dissésseis, dissessem

6. FUT. SUBJ.:   *disser, disseres, disser, dissermos,*
disserdes, disserem

7. FUT. IND.:   *direi, dirás, dirá, diremos, direis, dirão*

8. COND.:   *diria, dirias, diria, diríamos, diríeis,*
diriam

9. PAST. PART.:   *dito*

---

[1] *dêmos* Ⓟ.

Eleger to elect

1. PAST. PART.: *elegido* and *eleito*

Erigir to erect

1. PAST PART.: *erigido* and *ereto*

Escrever to write

1. PAST PART.: *escrito*

Estar to be

1. PRES. IND.: *estou, estás, está, estamos, estais, estão*
2. PRES. SUBJ.: *esteja, estejas, esteja, estejamos, estejais, estejam*
3. PRET. IND.: *estive, estiveste, estêve,[1] estivemos, estivestes, estiveram*
4. PLUP. IND.: *estivera, estiveras, estivera, estivéramos, estivéreis, estiveram*
5. IMP. SUBJ.: *estivesse, estivesses, estivesse, estivéssemos, estivésseis, estivessem*
6. FUT. SUBJ.: *estiver, estiveres, estiver, estivermos, estiverdes, estiverem*

Extinguir to extinguish

1. PAST PART.: *extinguido* and *extinto*

Fazer to do, to make

1. PRES. IND.: *faço, fazes, faz, fazemos, fazeis, fazem*
2. PRES. SUBJ.: *faça, faças, faça, façamos, façais, façam*

3. PRET. IND.:   *fiz, fizeste, fêz,*[1] *fizemos, fizestes,*
                      fizeram

4. PLUP. IND.:   *fizera, fizeras, fizera, fizéramos,*
                      fizéreis, fizeram

5. IMPF. SUBJ.:   *fizesse, fizesses, fizesse, fizéssemos,*
                      fizésseis, fizessem

6. FUT. SUBJ.:   *fizer, fizeres, fizer, fizermos, fizerdes,*
                      fizerem

7. FUT. IND.:   *farei, farás, fará, faremos, fareis, farão*

8. COND.:   *faria, farias, faria, faríamos, faríeis,*
                      fariam

9. PAST PART.:   *feito*

Haver to have

1. PRES. IND.:   *hei, hás, há, havemos, haveis, hão*

2. PRES. SUBJ.:   *haja, hajas, haja, hajamos, hajais,*
                      hajam

3. PRET. IND.:   *houve, houveste, houve, houvemos,*
                      houvestes, houveram

4. PLUP. IND.:   *houvera, houveras, houvera,*
                      houvéramos, houvéreis, houveram

5. IMPF. SUBJ.:   *houvesse, houvesses, houvesse,*
                      houvéssemos, houvésseis, houvessem

6. FUT. SUBJ.:   *houver, houveres, houver, houvermos,*
                      houverdes, houverem

Ir to go

1. PRES. IND.:   *vou, vais, vai, vamos, ides, vão*

2. PRES. SUBJ.:   *vá, vás, vá, vamos, vades, vão*

---

[1] *fez* Ⓟ.

3. IMPF. IND.: *ia, ias, ia, íamos, íeis, iam*

4. PRET. IND.: *fui, fôste,[1] foi, fomos, fôstes, foram*

5. PLUP. IND.: *fôra,[2] foras, fôra, fôramos, fôreis, foram*

6. IMPF. SUBJ.: *fôsse,[2] fôsses, fôsse, fôssemos, fôsseis, fôssem*

7. FUT. SUBJ.: *fôr,[3] fores, fôr,[3] formos, fordes, forem*

Ler to read

1. PRES. IND.: *leio, lês, lê, lemos, ledes, lêem*

2. PRES. SUBJ.: *leia, leias, leia, leiamos, leiais, leiam*

3. PRET. IND.: *li, lêste,[3] leu, lemos, lêstes,[3] leram*

Medir to measure

1. PRES. IND.: *meço, medes, mede, medimos, medis, medem*

2. PRES. SUBJ.: *meça, meças, meça, meçamos, meçais, meçam*

Ouvir to hear

1. PRES. IND.: *ouço, ouves, ouve, ouvimos, ouvis, ouvem*

also

PRES. IND.: *oiço, ouves, ouve, ouvimos, ouvis, ouvem*

2. PRES. SUBJ.: *ouça, ouças, ouça, ouçamos, ouçais, ouçam*

also

PRES. SUBJ.: *oiça, oiças, oiça, oiçamos, oiçais, oiçam*

---

[1] *foste, fostes,* Ⓟ

[2] No accent mark except in first and second plural forms Ⓟ

[3] No accent mark in Portugal.

Pedir to ask

1. PRES. IND.: *peço, pedes, pede, pedimos, pedis, pedem*

2. PRES. SUBJ.: *peça, peças, peça, peçamos, peçais, peçam*

Perder to lose

1. PRES. IND.: *perco, perdes, perde, perdemos, perdeis, perdem*

2. PRES. SUBJ.: *perca, percas, perca, percamos, percais, percam*

Poder to be able

1. PRES. IND.: *posso, podes, pode, podemos, podeis, podem*

2. PRES. SUBJ.: *possa, possas, possa, possamos, possais, possam*

3. PRET. IND.: *pude, pudeste, pôde, pudemos, pudestes, puderam*

4. PLUP. IND.: *pudera, puderas, pudera, pudéramos, pudéreis, puderam*

5. IMPF. SUBJ.: *pudesse, pudesses, pudesse, pudéssemos, pudésseis, pudessem*

6. FUT. SUBJ.: *puder, puderes, puder, pudermos, puderdes, puderem*

Pôr to put

1. PRES. IND.: *ponho, pões, põe, pomos, pondes, põem*

2. PRES. SUBJ.: *ponha, ponhas, ponha, ponhamos, ponhais, ponham*

3. IMPF. IND.: *punha, punhas, punha, púnhamos, púnheis, punham*

4. PRET. IND.: *pus, pusestę, pôs, pusemos, pusestes, puseram*

5. PLUP. IND.: *pusera, puseras, pusera, puséramos, puséreis, puseram*

6. IMPF. SUBJ.: *pusesse, pusesses, pusesse, puséssemos, pusésseis, pusessem*

7. FUT. SUBJ.: *puser, puseres, puser, pusermos, puserdes, puserem*

8. PAST. PART.: *pôsto (posto Ⓟ)*

9. PRES. PART.: *pondo*

Note: *compor* and other verbs formed from *pôr* will have the same irregularities as *pôr*.

Querer to want

1. PRES. IND.: *quero, queres, quer* or *quere,*[1] *queremos, quereis, querem*

2. PRES. SUBJ.: *queira, queiras, queira, queiramos, queirais, queiram*

3. PRET. IND.: *quis, quiseste, quis, quisemos, quisestes, quiseram*

4. PLUP. IND.: *quisera, quiseras, quisera, quiséramos, quiséreis, quiseram*

5. IMP. SUBJ.: *quisesse, quisesses, quisesse, quiséssemos, quisésseis, quisessem*

6. FUT. SUBJ.: *quiser, quiseres, quiser, quisermos, quiserdes, quiserem*

---

[1]Also used in Portugal, but *quer* is preferred under the new orthography.

Rir to laugh

1. PRES. IND.: *rio, ris, ri, rimos, rides, riem*
2. PRES. SUBJ.: *ria, rias, ria, riamos, riais, riam*

Saber to know

1. PRES. IND.: *sei, sabes, sabe, sabemos, sabeis, sabem*
2. PRES. SUBJ.: *saiba, saibas, saiba, saibamos, saibais, saibam*
3. PRET. IND.: *soube, soubeste, soube, soubemos, soubestes, souberam*
4. PLUP. IND.: *soubera, souberas, soubera, soubéramos, soubéreis, souberam*
5. IMPF. SUBJ.: *soubesse, soubesses, soubesse, soubéssemos, soubésseis, soubessem*
6. FUT. SUBJ.: *souber, souberes, souber, soubermos, souberdes, souberem*

Sair to go out, to leave

1. PRES. IND.: *saio, sais, sai, saímos, saís, saem*
2. PRES. SUBJ.: *saia, saias, saia, saiamos, saias, saiam*
3. IMPF. IND.: *saía, saías, saía, saíamos, saíeis, saíam*
4. PRET. IND.: *saí, saíste, saiu, saímos, saístes, saíram*
5. PLUP. IND.: *saíra, saíras, saíra, saíramos, saíreis, saíram*
6. IMPF. SUBJ.: *saísse, saísses, saísse, saíssemos, saísseis, saíssem*

7. FUT. SUBJ.: *sair, saíres, sair, sairmos, saírdes, saírem*

8. PAST PART.: *saído*

Ser to be

1. PRES. IND.: *sou, és, é, somos, sois, são*

2. PRES. SUBJ.: *seja, sejas, seja, sejamos, sejais, sejam*

3. IMPF. IND.: *era, eras, era, éramos, éreis, eram*

4. PRET. IND.: *fui, fôste,[1] foi, fomos, fôstes,[1] foram*

5. PLUP. IND.: *fôra,[2] foras, fôra, fôramos, fôreis, foram*

6. IMPF. SUBJ.: *fôsse,[2] fôsses, fôsse, fôssemos, fôsseis, fôssem*

7. FUT. SUBJ.: *fôr,[1] fores, fôr,[1] formos, fordes, forem*

Ter to have

1. PRES. IND.: *tenho, tens, tem, temos, tendes, têm*

2. PRES. SUBJ.: *tenha, tenhas, tenha, tenhamos, tenhais, tenham*

3. IMPF. IND.: *tinha, tinhas, tinha, tínhamos, tínheis, tinham*

4. PRET. IND.: *tive, tiveste, teve, tivemos, tivestes, tiveram*

5. PLUP. IND.: *tivera, tiveras, tivera, tivéramos, tivéreis, tiveram*

6. IMPF. SUBJ.: *tivesse, tivesses, tivesse, tivéssemos, tivésseis, tivessem*

---

[1] *foste, fostes;* for Ⓟ.

[2] No accent mark except in first and second plural forms Ⓟ.

7. FUT. SUBJ.: *tiver, tiveres, tiver, tivermos, tiverdes, tiverem*

Note: *conter* and other verbs formed from *ter* will have the same irregularities as *ter*.

Trazer to bring

1. PRES. IND.: *trago, trazes, traz, trazemos, trazeis, trazem*

2. PRES. SUBJ.: *traga, tragas, traga, tragamos, tragais, tragam*

3. PRET. IND.: *trouxe,[1] trouxeste, trouxe, trouxemos, trouxestes, trouxeram*

4. PLUP. IND.: *trouxera, trouxeras, trouxera, trouxéramos, trouxéreis, trouxeram*

5. IMPF. SUBJ.: *trouxesse, trouxesses, trouxesse, trouxéssemos, trouxésseis, trouxessem*

6. FUT. SUBJ.: *trouxer, trouxeres, trouxer, trouxermos, trouxerdes, trouxerem*

7. FUT. IND.: *trarei, trarás, trará, traremos, trareis, trarão*

8. COND.: *traria, trarias, traria, traríamos, traríeis, trariam*

Valer to be worth

1. PRES. IND.: *valho, vales, vale, valemos, valeis, valem*

2. PRES. SUBJ.: *valha, valhas, valha, valhamos, valhais, valham*

---

[1] In these verb forms *x* is pronounced like *s* in *see*.

Ver to see

1. PRES. IND.: *vejo, vês, vê, vemos, vêdes,*[1] *vêem*
2. PRES. SUBJ.: *veja, vejas, veja, vejamos, vejais, vejam*
3. PRET. IND.: *vi, viste, viu, vimos, vistes, viram*
4. PLUP. IND.: *vira, viras, vira, víramos, víreis, viram*
5. IMPF. SUBJ.: *visse, visses, visse, víssemos, vísseis, vissem*
6. FUT. SUBJ.: *vir, vires, vir, virmos, virdes, virem*
7. PAST PART: *visto*

Vir to come

1. PRES. IND.: *venho, vens, vem, vimos, vindes, vêm*
2. PRES. SUBJ.: *venha, venhas, venha, venhamos, venhais, venham*
3. IMPF. IND.: *vinha, vinhas, vinha, vínhamos, vínheis, vinham*
4. PRET. IND.: *vim, vieste, veio, viemos, viestes, vieram*
5. PLUP. IND.: *viera, vieras, viera, viéramos, viéreis, vieram*
6. IMPF. SUBJ.: *viesse, viesses, viesse, viéssemos, viésseis, viessem*
7. FUT. SUBJ.: *vier, vieres, vier, viermos, vierdes, vierem*
8. PAST PART.: *vindo*

Note: The present participle is also *vindo.*

Note: *convir* to suit, to agree, and other verbs formed from *vir,* will have the same irregularities as *vir.*

---

[1] *vedes* Ⓟ.

1. FORMAL INVITATIONS
AND REPLIES

A.

Pedro Pereira Sousa e Maria Sousa têm o prazer de convidar V. Excia. e Exma. Família para assistirem ao enlace matrimonial de (da) sua filha Glória com o Sr. Paulo Gomes, que se realizará na igreja de Santo Antônio[1] no dia 20 do corrente, às 18 horas. Depois da cerimônia,[2] haverá uma recepção na casa dos pais da noiva, à avenida Anchieta, 1529.

Peter Pereira Sousa and Mary Sousa take pleasure in inviting you to the wedding of their daughter Gloria to Mr. Paulo Gomes, which will take place at St. Anthony's Church on the 20th of this month at 6 p. m. After the ceremony there will be a reception at the residence of the bride's parents, 1529 Anchieta Avenue.

———

B.

José e Cecília Silva cumprimentam o senhor e a senhora Carlos Guimarães, e pedem que os honrem jantando na sua companhia, na próxima segunda-feira, às oito horas.

Joseph and Cecilia Silva extend their greetings to Mr. and Mrs. Charles Guimarães, and would be honored to have their company at dinner next Monday at eight o'clock.

———

———

[1] António Ⓟ.
[2] *cerimónia* Ⓟ.

O senhor e a senhora Guimarães, muito agradecidos, aceitam com grande prazer o convite do senhor e da senhora Silva para jantarem juntos na próxima segunda-feira, às oito horas, e aproveitam o ensejo para cumprimentá-los cordialmente.

Mr. and Mrs. Guimarães will be delighted to dine with Mr. and Mrs. Silva next Monday at eight o'clock and take this opportunity to indicate their appreciation and to extend their kindest regards.

———————

O senhor e a senhora Guimarães cumprimentam o senhor e a senhora Silva, agradecem muitíssimo o seu amável convite para jantar na próxima segunda-feira, mas lamentam não poderem aceitá-lo em virtude de já terem estabelecido um compromisso anteriormente, para a mesma data.

Mr. and Mrs. Guimarães extend their greetings to Mr. and Mrs. Silva and thank them for the kind invitation to dine with them on Monday, but regret that they will not be able to come due to a previous engagement.

———————

O senhor e a senhora Moreira da Silva agradecem muito o amável convite do senhor e da senhora Freitas, e expressam o seu grande contentamento por terem a oportunidade de participar da festa do próximo domingo.

Mr. and Mrs. Moreira da Silva gratefully acknowledge the kind invitation of Mr. and Mrs. Freitas and

will be most happy to attend the reception next
Sunday.

C.

Tomás e Margarida Freitas cumprimentam afetuo-
samente o senhor e a senhora Moreira da Silva e
pedem que lhes dêem o grande prazer de participarem
da festa com que comemorarão o aniversário de (da)
sua filha Ana, festa essa que terá lugar no próximo
domingo, 19 de março,[1] às nove horas da noite.

Thomas and Margaret Freitas extend their warm-
est greetings to Mr. and Mrs. Moreira da Silva and
request the honor of their presence at a party cele-
brating the birthday of their daughter Ana, to be given
on Sunday evening, March 19, at nine o'clock.

---

[1] Março Ⓟ.

2. THANK-YOU NOTE

2 de abril[1] de 1965

Minha cara Ana,

Escrevo-lhe não só para cumprimentá-la, como também para agradecer-lhe o formoso vaso que me mandou de presente. Coloquei-o em cima do piano, e você não pode imaginar o lindo efeito que faz.

Espero vê-la, amanhã, na festa que dá Carlota. Parece que essa reunião vai ser muito animada.

Meu desejo é que você e tôda[2] a família estejam bem. Aqui, tudo sem novidade.

Abraça-a (a) sua amiga dedicada.

Maria

April 2, 1965

Dear Anna,

I'm writing you not only to say hello, but also to let you know how much I appreciate the beautiful vase you sent me as a gift. I've put it on the piano and you can't imagine the beautiful effect.

I hope to see you at Carlota's party tomorrow. I think it's going to be a very lively affair.

I hope you and your family are well. Here, everything is fine.

Your friend,
Mary

----

[1] Abril ℗.
[2] toda ℗.

3. BUSINESS LETTERS

B.   Rua Tobias Barreto, 1326
                            São Paulo, S. P.
                            5 de julho[1] de 1965

Sr. Júlio Matos
Avenida Rio Branco, 213
Rio de Janeiro
Estado de Guanabara

Ilmo. Snr:

   Junto remeto-lhe um cheque de Cr$3.000,00 para
obtenção de uma assinatura anual da revista *Branco
e Negro,* que é dirigida por V. S.[2]

                            Atenciosamente,
                               João Carlos Martins

                            _____

                            Rua Tobias Barreto, 1326
                            São Paulo, S. P.
                            July 5, 1965

Mr. Júlio Matos
Avenida Rio Branco, 213
Rio de Janeiro
Guanabara State

Dear Sir:

   Enclosed please find a check for 3000 cruzeiros for
a year's subscription to your magazine *Branco e Negro.*
                            Very truly yours,
                               João Carlos Martins

_____
   [1] Julho Ⓟ.
   [2] V. S. stands for Vossa Senhoria, a correspondence term
for "you."

A.

> Lopes, Nunes & Cia.
> Rua de Madalena, 154
> Lisboa, Portugal
>
> 2 de Maio[1] de 1965

Aos Snrs.
Gomes, Lima & Cia.
Rua Nova d'Alfândega, 110
o Porto[2]

Prezados Senhores:

Temos a satisfação de apresentar-lhes o portador desta, o Sr. Alberto Rocha, nosso caixeiro viajante, que visitará as principais cidades dessa região.

Não é preciso dizer-lhes que ficaremos imensamente gratos pelas atenções que lhe dispensarem.

Aproveitamos a oportunidade para agradecer-lhes antecipadamente o que fizerem pelo Sr. Rocha, e subscrevemo-nos muito atenciosamente.

> De VV. SS.
> Atos. e Obos.
>
> Lopes, Nunes & Cia.
>
> João Lopes
> Presidente

---

[1] maio Ⓑ.
[2] Pôrto. Ⓑ

Lopes, Nunes & Co.
Rua de Madalena, 154
Lisbon, Portugal

May 2, 1965

Gomes, Lima & Co.
Rua Nova d'Alfândega, 110
o Porto

Gentlemen:

We have the pleasure of introducing to you the bearer of this letter, Mr. Alberto Rocha, our traveling salesman, who will be visiting the principal cities of your region.

Needless to say, we shall greatly appreciate any courtesy you may extend to him.

Thanking you in advance, we remain

Very truly yours,
Lopes, Nunes & Cia.

João Lopes
President

4. INFORMAL LETTERS

2 de fevereiro[1]

Meu caro José,

Foi com grande prazer que recebi a sua última carta. Para ir direito ao assunto, vou contar-lhe a grande notícia. Finalmente decidimos fazer a projetada (projectada) viagem a Lisboa, onde pretendemos ficar todo o mês de julho.

Naturalmente Maria está encantada, muito ansiosa de visitar o país dos seus avós e de conhecer você e sua amável espôsa.[2] Estou certo de que ela e Helena se darão bem aí, e que aproveitarão tôdas[2] as horas, visitando os pontos de interêsse[2] da cidade, e não esquecendo, naturalmente, as lojas, onde se dedicarão à "arte" de fazer compras. Temos muitas coisas que comentar e espero que você possa livrar-se de outros compromissos durante êsses[2] dias.

Os negócios vão bem por agora e espero que continuem assim, de vento em pôpa.[2] Na semana passada estive com o Alberto, e êle perguntou por você.

Ficarei muito agradecido se você puder reservar-nos um quarto num hotel, pertinho do prédio em que mora.

Escreva-me, contando o que tem acontecido ùltimamente, e o que lhe parece esta notícia.

Mando lembranças a Helena, e você, receba um abraço de (do) seu amigo

João

---

[1] Fevereiro Ⓟ.
[2] No accent mark in Portugal: esposa, etc.

February 2

Dear Joseph,

I was very happy to get your last letter. Without further delay I'm going to spring the big news. We have finally decided to take the trip to Lisbon, where we expect to spend all of July.

Naturally, Mary is delighted, being most anxious to visit the country of her grandparents and to meet you and your charming wife. I am sure that she and Helen will get along fine and that they will put their time to good use, visiting points of interest in the city, not forgetting, of course, the shops, where they can practice their shopping "art." We have much to talk about and I hope you will be able to free yourself of other engagements during that period.

Business is good now and I hope we shall continue to have smooth sailing. I saw Al last week and he asked about you.

I'd appreciate it very much if you could reserve a room for us in a hotel near the building in which you are staying.

Write, letting me know what has been going on lately and what you think of the news.

Give my regards to Helen.

Yours,

John

5. USEFUL PHRASES FOR CORRESPONDENCE

A. FORMAL LETTERS

1. Salutations:

Excelentíssimo Senhor:	Dear Sir: (Your Excellency)
Amigo e Senhor:	Dear Sir:
Ilustríssimo Senhor:	Dear Sir:
Prezado Senhor:	Dear Sir:
Senhor:	Sir:
Senhora:	Madam:
Senhorita:	Miss:
Senhor Diretor:[1]	Dear Director:

Note: The above phrases can be used in the plural: *Excelentíssimos Senhores, Amigos e Senhores,* etc., and in the feminine: *Excelentíssima Senhora, Amiga e Senhora,* etc. They can also be used with names:

Prezado Senhor Pereira: Dear Mr. Pereira:

2. Initial or opening statements:

Acusamos o recebimento de (do) seu estimado favor de 12 dêste[2] e aproveitamo-nos para . . . We hereby acknowledge receipt of your letter of the 12th instant and take this opportunity to. . .

Agradecemos o seu atencioso favor, datado de 7 do mês corrente . . . We greatly appreciate your kind letter of the 7th of this month . . .

---

[1] Director Ⓟ.
[2] No accent mark in Portugal.

Cumpre-nos anunciar-lhes que . . . Please be advised that . . .

É com grande prazer que respondo à sua estimada carta . . . I take pleasure in answering your letter . . .

Em resposta à carta de VV. SS.[1] de 28 do mês passado, cumpre-nos informar-lhes que . . . In answer to your letter of the 28th of last month, please be advised that . . .

Estou em posse de (do) seu prezado favor de 22 de junho[2] e cumpre-me avisá-lo que . . . I am in receipt of your letter of June 22 and am pleased to inform you that . . .

Muito grato ficaria a V. S. se me mandasse . . . I would appreciate it very much if you would send me . . .

Recebi (a) sua estimada carta de 15 do corrente e apresso-me a . . . I have received your letter of the 15th of this month and I hasten to . . .

Temos a satisfação de comunicar-lhe que . . . We are pleased to announce that . . .

3. Closing statements:

More formal:

Apresento-lhes os meus sinceros cumprimentos de muita estima

Aproveitamos o ensejo para lhes renovarmos os nossos protestos de elevada consideração e estima

---

[1] VV. SS. stands for Vossas Senhorias, "you" plural; de VV. SS. "your."

[2] Junho Ⓟ.

Com os nossos protestos de sincera estima e elevado aprêço,[1] subscrevemo-nos

Subscrevemo-nos com alta estima e consideração

Note: These are roughly the equivalent of "Sincerely yours."

More commercial:

Com alta estima e consideração

Desde já, muito gratos, somos, atenciosamente

Somos com tôda[1] a consideração

Note: These amount to "Very truly yours."

Com os nossos atenciosos cumprimentos . . . With our best regards . . .

Na expectativa de uma breve resposta . . . Hoping to hear from you soon . . .

Na esperança de recebermos seus comentários favoráveis . . . Hoping to receive a favorable response . . .

Respeitosamente . . . Respectfully . . .

The above may be followed by phrases such as the following which correspond to our "Very truly yours," or "Sincerely yours":

De Vossa Senhoria	De V. S.
Atento e Obrigado	Ato. e Obgdo.
De Vossas Senhorias	De VV. SS.
Amigos e Muito Gratos	Amos. e Mto. Gtos.

---

[1] No accent mark in Portugal.

Note: These are usually given in the abbreviated forms given to the right; the shortened forms vary, so Obrigado may appear as Obo., etc. The combinations also vary:

Muito Atentos e Gratos, etc.

B. INFORMAL LETTERS

1. Salutations:

Amigo Carlos	My friend Charles
Meu caro Alberto	My dear Albert
Meu prezado Amigo	My dear Friend
Minha boa Carmen	My dear ("good") Carmen
Minha filha querida	My dearest daughter
Minha querida Cecília	My dear Cecilia
Prezado Amigo	Dear Friend
Prezado Alfredo	Dear Alfred
Prezada Maria	Dear Mary
Querida Mamãe	Dearest Mother
Querida sobrinha	Dear Niece

2. Complimentary closings:

Abraça-o o amigo
Aceite abraço muito sincero do amigo dedicado
Aceite os cumprimentos sinceros do amigo
Do amigo dedicado
Envia-lhe um apertado abraço a sincera amiga
Recebam um abraço do seu
Seu amigo muito grato
Um abraço do seu

Note: These phrases above amount to "Yours,"
"Affectionately yours," or corresponding expressions.

Até a vista	Until I see you again
Cordialmente	Cordially
Seu filho muito dedicado	Your loving son

6. FORM OF THE ENVELOPE

Lopes, Nunes & Cia.
Rua de Madalena, 154
Lisboa

    Aos Srs.
    Gomes, Lima & Cia.
    Rua Nova d'Alfândega, 110
    O PORTO[1]

João Carlos Martins
Rua Tobias Barreto, 1326
São Paulo, S. P.

    Ilmo. Snr.
    Júlio Matos
    Avenida Rio Branco, 213
    RIO DE JANEIRO, Guanabara

---

[1] Pôrto Ⓑ.

Ilmo. Snr.
José Pereira Martins
Rua Castilho, 73
LISBOA, PORTUGAL

João Santos
Praia do Flamengo, 376
RIO DE JANEIRO
GUANABARA

OTHER EXAMPLES

Exmo. Sr. Dr. Carlos de Silveira
Praça da Sé, 379
SÃO PAULO, S. P.

Snra. Carmen Pereira
Avenida Rui Barbosa, 322
RIO DE JANEIRO, GUANABARA

Snrta. Maria da Silva
Av. P. A. Cabral, 92
LISBOA, PORTUGAL